NOT A VICTIM
BUT A WARRIOR

MARK WINN

Winn, Mark. *Not a Victim But A Warrior*

Copyright © 2021 by Mark Winn

Published by KWE Publishing: www.kwepub.com

ISBN 978-1-950306-23-7 (paperback) 978-1-950306-24-4 (ebook)

Library of Congress Control Number: 2020914074

1. Business Leadership 2. Business & Organizational Learning 3. Martial Arts (books)

CONTENTS

ACKNOWLEDGMENTS

I would like to thank Kimberley Eley and her team at KWE Publishing as this book was a labor of love and her team was tremendous in going from concept to final product.

I would like to thank my Krav Maga instructors – David Rubinberg 8th Dan in KAPAP Krav Maga under Grandmaster Avi Nardia, Master Bruce Rubinberg who has always been there for my success in training, and mentoring by Israeli Defense Forces Retired Major and Grandmaster Avi Nardia.

I would also like to thank all of my martial arts

instructors who have added so much to my journey in training and outlook in life.

I would like to thank my students and family for the inspiration to write this book as there are so many aspects of defending ourselves physically and mentally. I honestly believe that we are placed on this earth to help each other.

FOREWORD

It is with much enthusiasm that I recommend Mark Winn's new book as your next read.

I was one of Mark's instructors for multiple Kapap Krav Maga classes during his training in the USA.

Mark Winn has displayed a level of creativity, wit, and analytical thought that is quite unique and transported it to his writing that I am sure will be an inspiration for the current and future generations of martial artists.

Avi Nardia, retired Major, IDF, Founder KAPAP Krav Maga

INTRODUCTION

While most of us avoid thinking about it, I'd like you to consider that at any given time, we are exposed to a multitude of threats, stimuli, and opportunities. In your daily life, some of you will recognize these threats right away. Others of you may not recognize these threats initially, and as a result, they can take you by surprise. What you don't know can easily blindside you in life.

How can you identify what you can't see?

As an insurance agent and as a Krav Maga martial arts instructor, my purpose in life is to provide individuals the tools and a path to decrease their chances of becoming a victim and seeing what may appear to be hidden. I am all about protecting my clients' assets and empowering them to protect themselves physically. In this book, I want to share my expertise from both of my fields so I can teach you to live as a warrior.

Through strategies, both material and mental, you will learn to increase your ability to survive not only a physical attack but a mental one. Even in unfamiliar situations, you will learn to observe potential threats you may have ignored or dismissed previously. Once you identify these situations, you will discover ways to handle and neutralize the threats.

Through thirty years of martial arts training, I have gained many strategies and obtained wisdom from my teachers, mentors, and other resources. I am an instructor trained in Krav Maga, a dynamic and combative Israeli self-defense and fighting system. Through my years of experience, I have observed that what I teach on the mats in the gym can also be applied to our daily lives at work, at school, at church, and at home. In the upcoming chapters, I invite you to look at these examples and consider how you can transform these teachings into lessons you can use in all areas of your life. In Krav Maga class, I teach my students in order to make them successful in a self-defense situation. In this book, my goal is to teach you these concepts to enable you to become successful in your life.

MarkWinn, Krav Maga instructor with close to thirty years of martial arts training, is demonstrating a knife disarm.

All of us know people who have achieved excellence in one area of their lives but are totally "upside-down" in other aspects. Here are a couple of examples you may recognize:

- When you were in high school, did you know an athlete who worked extremely hard to excel in their sport, but did not focus on their academics? Did you notice this athlete putting in extra time in their practice and training, but refusing to seek help to become an outstanding scholar?
- Have you met a person who excels in their career in corporate America, but their home life is a total mess?

While the athlete and business person in these examples appear to look like winners in one arena, they are losers in other crucial areas of their lives. Common wisdom says you should not trust a martial artist who achieves a black belt level of training but doesn't apply the same discipline to the other aspects of their life. As one of my friends, Master Michael Bugg, once said, "You shouldn't be a black belt and drive a Chevette," meaning we should aim to excel in all facets of our lives, not just one.

In this book, I will talk about the difference between victims and warriors. What do you think about when you hear the words "victim" and "warrior"? Often people think of a victim as someone who was taken advantage of, was caught off guard, or who put themselves in the wrong place at the wrong time. When people think of a warrior, they frequently envision someone who is a fighter, and a winner who overcomes.

Through this book, I will challenge you to reconsider these definitions.

Usually, a victim is defined as a person harmed, injured, or killed in a crime, accident, or other event or action. In other words, a victim is a person who is tricked or duped. In this book, we are looking at the meaning of the word "victim" from the aspect of someone who could be harmed, and a victim situation is an opportunity in which harm could occur.

The definition of a warrior is a brave or experienced soldier or fighter. It is a person engaged or seasoned in warfare broadly: a person involved in some struggle or conflict. In this book, I will use the definition I received from Avi Nardia, an expert martial artist in the hand to hand combat systems Kapap Lotar and Brazilian Jiu-Jitsu, who was in the special forces, anti-terrorist unit, and is a master martial artist. He describes a warrior as someone who protects himself and those behind him.

To me, Avi's quote means this: If we are protecting our bodies, minds, and spirits against the struggle and conflict in life, we are warriors.

Why do I define a warrior and victim this way? If you don't look at life with an open eye, you will become a victim of your own actions, your failure to act, or your inability to see a threat. As a warrior, you are vigilant to your surroundings in order to go home safely. This is not just for your personal safety but also so you can return to the people who count on you. As you will see, striving to avoid being a victim and becoming a warrior is goal-oriented, not situational.

As you learn actual martial arts techniques in this book, and as I relate these moves to the everyday lessons you can learn from these moves, you will be able to more effectively protect yourself through the concepts I am sharing. Another quote that Avi Nardia shared is, "If I teach you a technique, you will have a technique, but if I teach you a concept, you will have 1,000 techniques." This is a powerful mindset, as having a technique as a foundation will enable you to create new ways of tackling and succeeding in new challenges.

Let's look at some of the concepts you will learn:

How do I become a protector instead of the one who always needs protecting?

Ask yourself: Do you always need someone else to protect you, cover you, and to step up and act as your savior in a crisis? If so, I will show how you can change your mindset and your destiny.

How can I create a maximum impact?

Too often we underestimate our abilities because we

don't understand what we have the power to do. I will define what a maximum impact is and describe ways you can analyze a situation.

How can I create a minimal risk for myself?

Self-defense situations are not without danger, but there are ways to minimize your risks through the ways, means, and methods you choose. I will look at self-defense moves that create a minimal risk, and compare these to the choices we make every day.

What is the OODA loop and how can I use it?

I'll introduce you to the OODA Loop, a strategic method of thinking which has been successfully employed by the military. We will study how using the OODA loop will help you survive, avoid and evade an attack in self-defense and in your daily life.

What is Kadima and how can I use it to be successful in attacks?

Kadima is the Hebrew word for forward and is an important concept in the context of Krav Maga. I will explain what Kadima is and talk about how you can use Kadima to become a warrior.

What does being the Gray Man have to do with my ability to defend myself?

Being the Gray Man means camouflaging yourself in a crowd. You will learn that drawing attention to yourself can bring unwanted danger into your life. I will discuss how you can avoid being noticed and use it to your advantage to survive.

What does "being like water" mean?

I will explain what it means to be like water, and why

we want to strive to be like water. I will discuss how being like water is about mindfulness, and ways you can apply this mindset in your life.

What are Mu Ying and Yow Ying?

Mu Ying and Yow Ying are concepts in martial arts. In order to become a warrior, you must learn how someone's ability to move can enable you to better protect yourself. I will explain how you can become malleable in your life by using Mu Ying and Yow Ying so you can adapt.

How can I live life unafraid?

It's natural to experience fear at times in our lives. As humans, we have always discovered more by exploration which means we must face our anxieties. The trials and tribulations are what create the strongest impact on our progress. I will show how you can change your outlook by living unafraid.

What is the real trick of close-up magic?

Have you ever observed a magician and wondered how their tricks worked? Often the things we see aren't what they seem. I will explain how practicing having a more watchful eye will empower you to win in all aspects of your life.

How can I build armor?

Armor is protection we wear or use to keep from becoming a victim. It doesn't matter what your body composition or lifestyle is, as there is always something we can do to improve our ability to have stronger armor in self-defense. I will discuss how this applies to everyday situations in our lives, too.

How do I take the opponent's "real estate"?

I'll explain what it means in martial arts to take an opponent's "real estate." In life and in the gym, we may think we are handling a situation and gaining ground, only to turn around and lose it. When this happens, have we really accomplished our goal? I'll discuss this and more.

How does this all tie together and "live on red"?

I will introduce you to what it means to "live on red" in order to bring all of these concepts together by recapping. You'll learn how to employ everything you cover in this book so you can live the very best life you can.

CHAPTER 1 - HOW DO I BECOME A PROTECTOR INSTEAD OF THE ONE WHO ALWAYS NEEDS PROTECTING?

Have you ever considered that throughout your life, from the time you were a baby until now, you have had people looking after you? This includes family, extended family, friends, teachers, law enforcement, and on a larger scale, our military. We have people protecting our nation, our neighborhoods, our bodies, and our emotions. Some would even say these same people are trying to protect our future.

From this standpoint or approach to life, we seem to have a lot of safeguards around us. But is that actually true? Are we always being protected? Consider the fact that we as people fall down, get injured, robbed, attacked, or pursued all of the time. While we can't stop everything that happens to us, with the right safeguards in our lives, often we're in a better position. For many of us, our everyday existence appears to be pretty safe.

Much of that feeling of safety comes from how much trust we have in the people who protect us, and our ability to protect ourselves. This influences how we show up in our lives every day. Here are some examples:

- Have you ever known someone who acts totally helpless and seems not to be able to do anything without the security of someone else helping them?
- Have you ever known someone who was scared to leave their home due to past experiences or paranoia?
- On the flip side, have you ever known a person who walks around feeling invulnerable to anything possibly occurring to them?

Are you showing up in your life in a way that is clueless, freaked out, or confident?

What do the examples show? They demonstrate that sometimes we are oblivious to what we need, or we overcompensate for what we need when it comes to our protection.

What level of risk are you willing to transfer to someone else? If you want the ability to protect yourself, then you need to know how to handle certain situations on your own. Why do you need to have the mental and physical ability to deal with threats that occur in life? The reason you want to have those abilities is because you may not always have someone available to assist you.

Think about a parent with a child. If the parent hovers over the child, and never allows them to be hurt, injured, or interact with others, how will the child grow or learn to protect themselves? If the parent doesn't allow the child to fail, to make mistakes, or to experience these events, will they adequately be able to protect themselves mentally and handle the pitfalls of life? Probably not.

Let's look at two examples.

One is an adult who is oblivious that anything can happen to them because nothing traumatic has ever happened to them. This person counts on the protection of others to keep them safe at all times. The fallacy in thinking like this person comes from the fact that number one, not everyone has goodwill towards us. Number two, the people that we use for protection will not always be with us. Number three, it is foolish to have a false sense of security or confidence that because nothing has happened to us previously that nothing ever will. Therefore, when this person is met by a menace, due to their lack of experience, they will often succumb to that threat. They will be taken off guard and therefore they are a victim.

Here's an example I have encountered frequently. I've met people who have a false sense of security because they took a single conceal and carry gun class. They have purchased a firearm which they only used one time on a range. Even though they have very limited experience, they feel they have the ability to retain their firearm and use it properly under threat. I have to say that these people are really setting themselves up for failure. In other words, they believe they have strength and safety on their side, but it is a false sense of security. If this person tries to act strong in a real crisis, based on their limited experience they may forget information they learned in their one and only firearms course. As a result, they could end up losing the firearm to someone who outmaneuvers them and takes their firearm from them. They may find out they are not really strong, and they will fall.

Now let's look at another type of person. This is a person who lives in constant fear about what could happen to them. Paralyzed by their fear, this person has "victim" written all over them. They will not move forward in life or make decisions unless they have a safety net. They refuse to take any risks at all unless they know that they are on safe ground.

The reason these examples are important to consider is that we do not want to build a false sense of confidence or protection. Nor do we want to spend our lives hiding and never taking any risks. We are better off training our minds and bodies to be able to protect ourselves and to continue practicing what we've learned. With training, you gain confidence and practical skills. It provides you with the knowledge and experience to address threats you may have in life without shutting down and not living your life at all.

This is not only important in self-protection, but in personal development, too. It is through experiencing life's challenges that we develop our strength. It has been said, to forge the greatest sword, you must heat it and beat out the impurities. Only then can it have the strength to perform what it was made to accomplish. Similarly, training and development of the mind are vital to becoming a protector of yourself. And frankly, you can't protect anyone else unless you can do this for yourself. We must develop our minds and techniques to survive the attacks of life.

Sometimes the desire to protect backfires. Earlier I mentioned hovering parents who are concerned about their children getting into harm's way while having the best of intentions. However, they can unintentionally prevent their children from being able to defend themselves. In my first book, *Grounded: Life Lessons*, I shared how plants that are grown hydroponically are weaker than plants grown in the field. Similarly, people who deal with the "elements" in their lives, the difficult situations, become stronger. Hovering parents are like hydroponics, keeping their children from the very challenges that would make them tougher. When children are allowed to develop their minds and truly deal with life versus justifying failure and mistakes, they grow into individuals with strength and courage.

These individuals who have strength and courage have real survival skills, as compared to just acting in a confident manner. Let's talk a little bit about the expression, "Fake it until you make it." There is a difference between working toward a strength or ability goal, and "playing opossum" by pretending you have a strength or ability goal before you have fully mastered it. From a work standpoint, if you try to act as though you know more than you do, you risk looking foolish. If someone who is an expert realizes you're not being authentic, it could be damaging to your reputation and your career. You would be better off in that case by pulling back a little and admitting what you don't know.

Another example is someone who feels safe complaining about poor service to a restaurant manager. When they complain to the manager, and the manager apologizes, the person starts to feel empowered. As a customer, the power is in their hands, as restaurants are a service industry that depend on pleasing their clients. But let's say this same person who complains believes they have the same power in every place that they go. This false sense of empowerment could put the person in real danger if they stand up for themselves to the wrong person. The person could let their power at the restaurant go to their head and assume they have it available to them in every situation. People who act this way may be putting themselves in peril.

Other examples of this are when people act bravely when they feel protected by a vehicle or an electronic device. While driving their vehicle, people may feel invincible. And others have "keyboard courage," feeling when they are online or on social media that they can type things they would not say if they were face to face with someone. Being behind the wheel and the keyboard creates a false sense of security. Many drivers who provoke "road rage" may find themselves followed and cornered by an angry driver. Similarly, sending posts "anonymously" is foolish as ugly comments can often be traced back to the poster. Yet every day, people post on things they shouldn't on social media, saying whatever they want to say in whatever way they want without thinking about the repercussions.

Any psychologist will tell you that it takes a process

to develop our minds and techniques. It is not a switch you can turn on or a pill you can take. When you think about this, know that it takes more than just a mindset. It takes time to develop the proper mental aptitude and physical technique to be successful as a warrior and survive an attack. The person who is willing to do the extra work it takes, however, has the power to change their life. These are the people who spend the extra time on the firearms range or in the gym mastering their martial arts techniques. The people who fail to do this will always be looking for someone else to save the day for them. They may blame systems or other people for not being there for them instead of taking responsibility for results. They are victims, not warriors.

CONFRONT YOURSELF
FOR YOURSELF

Jackie came from a loving family where everyone always had her back. As a young girl, she was soft-spoken and mild. Anytime kids would pick on her, there was always a sibling, teacher, or another adult to stand up for her and shield her from comments, insults, and attacks. As she got older in high school, there were fewer people protecting her from life and she began keeping to herself. As Jackie entered college, she almost didn't make it because social interaction became challenging. She would only do what she had to do to meet her class requirements. As a young adult, she avoided confrontations and made career decisions that placed her in positions of analysis versus interaction.

Jackie only felt comfortable working directly with her immediate group and at the end of her workday, she was only comfortable at home. Until one day at work, she had an "aha" moment. She started to realize that other people were no more talented or proficient than she was in order to surpass her to higher positions of promotion. She noticed one of the differences was their ability to communicate and interact with other departments. She felt her life was passing her by. This caused her to look at other areas of her life. She looked at family members she grew up with and friends that married and started families. She thought about what she could have and started to desire more in those areas of her life as well. Lastly, she reflected on how she avoided confrontation and interaction socially. This impacted her dating life, as well as her friendships. In both cases, her challenge with leaving her comfort zone became an obstacle to her having friends and dating. If she left her comfort zone, they saw her as codependent and clingy. She didn't feel that way about herself and didn't want others to see her that way either. Part of her history was to avoid confrontation and hideout for safety.

But fortunately, her desire to want something different got the best of her. Her "why" to improve her life and the opportunities she had been blessed with got bigger. She started to make changes and began developing herself. She started taking public speaking and joined an organization that would help her develop this skill set. Jackie decided to go to social gatherings with coworkers and friends, which allowed her to meet her future spouse but she still had the obstacle of confrontation. Then she overheard a friend discussing self-defense training. Her friend told her it was empowering from day one. The idea that she could actually do something effective in a self-defense situation changed her outlook and she wasn't shy anymore. Her friend admitted it took time to develop but she did it.

"If you do not conquer self, you will be conquered by self." – Napoleon Hill

Jackie realized she had to confront herself to win. She also found allies along the way to help her see just what she could do. Finally, she saw that she was the only person holding her back. At work, she started climbing the ladder and eventually became a director in her business unit. She trained in Krav Maga self-defense and became quite capable of handling various self-defense situations strategically, mentally, and physically. She went as far as saying it was the best physical shape she had ever been in, but she had to go through it to get to it. Moreover, she found the love of her life and they are happy supporting each other's dreams. She has been sharing her story by volunteering to mentor teenagers, as well as associates within her work organization. She became a self-defense instructor teaching both men and women to find the power within to deal with conflict. She has often quoted Imi Lichtenfeld, founder of Krav Maga who said, "We train so one may walk in peace."

She went through the process of changing her life and she no longer had to be the one protected. Jackie became the protector and created her destiny.

CHAPTER 2 – HOW CAN I CREATE A MAXIMUM IMPACT?

In the previous chapter, we learned that we need to think and act in a different way to become a protector. In this chapter, we will learn another way to become a protector: by making a maximum impact.

In self-defense, when you make an impact of any sort when fighting an opponent, it is vitally important to ensure it is effective. The more energy you bring to the strike, the more it disrupts, disables, or injures your attacker. Why is this important? If your attacker can't continue and becomes neutralized, you are safe. It is ineffective striking that escalates the likelihood of injury to you because the attacker will be able to further retaliate.

In practicing the dynamic self-defense and fighting system of Krav Maga, I teach my students to bring as much power to their technique as possible. Conveying as much energy and power from your body as you can is the most effective method. This is done through bursting (striking, blocking, and advancing at the same time), crashing (being able to close distance with power and technique to limit your attacker and become the aggressor), and having effective techniques. So, let's break these moves down.

Bursting allows you to protect yourself as you defend against an opponent while using effective striking surfaces such as hammer and palm strikes. While punching is an option, ask any boxer if they have ever sprained their wrist or broken something in their hand during a strike. Their answer will be yes! When I teach these strikes to my students, I always want to make sure that they can defend themselves effectively while avoiding injuries.

Retired Major Avi Nardia bursting with a palm strike.

Once you burst against an attack, you can then advance your response because often you have used a gross motor movement. One example of a gross motor movement is blocking your opponent using your entire arm versus only using your palm, which is more effective. A gross motor movement invokes less risk because you can block your opponent with maximum shielding.

The bursting movement provides opportunities to continue to defend and neutralize the attack. As you burst, you will advance your entire body forward in your movement against the limb that is coming at you. This is important because it allows you to bring more energy than you are receiving against the appendage that is attacking you.

Crashing using an elbow.

Crashing is the next maneuver that creates a maximum impact. I usually describe crashing as continuous techniques working together to neutralize an attack. That means you use a string of techniques performed in concert that limit your attacker's ability to defend against them, while at the same time shutting them down. This is different than other methods of self-defense because once you start crashing, everything works together towards one goal. I liken it to one train car coming behind the other until arrival.

You might be asking, what's the difference between

bursting and crashing? A burst is a defensive burst of action that occurs once, whereas a crash is a flurry of activity that is continual.

Effective techniques are the last aspect of creating a maximum impact. If you haven't pressure tested a particular technique to ensure it will work for you, you will not have a high success rate when using it under threat. As we all know, proficiency drops under a threat. In fact, in martial arts, if your techniques can't be performed under pressure to be successful at a rate of 70% or higher, you are better off learning another technique. Any technique with a rate of 50% or lower proficiency under pressure definitely should be avoided.

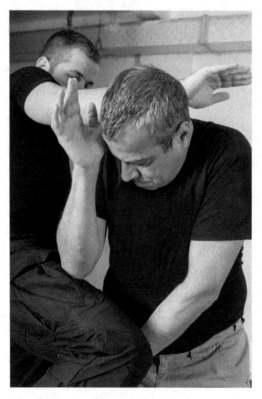

Avi Nardia using a gross motor movement to attack and shield.

There is one difference that I need to mention regarding these moves. If you use a gross motor movement like Krav Maga's 360 blocking or shielding techniques, this gives you a better opportunity to stop an initial attack versus a fine motor movement such as grabbing the wrist or using a fine movement to block.

Now let's look at how these concepts translate to other aspects of our lives. Knowing life is short and we will not live forever, we need to create the maximum impact that we can employ in our lives and the lives of others. Let's start with the last subject matter, technique.

In our everyday lives, technique speaks to our communication, thought processes, and our ability to change. If we are not deliberate in our communication, information can become lost or misconstrued and our connections will not be effective. Whether you are trying to ask for help, share information with someone, or let someone know you are there for them, you have to be deliberate in thought before you communicate these ideas. When it comes to your thought processes, you must be teachable and willing to grow if you are going to make a positive and maximum impact on those with whom you connect. If you stay pliable to change and open to communication, you will find that your techniques for dealing with life grow and improve your ability to surpass prior accomplishments.

So how does crashing apply to life? If you remember, crashing is a group of techniques that advances the goal of neutralizing an attack. It is not one thing or another, but a group of activities to reach this goal. The same way we use synergy of the body to complete a goal, we must use synergy of others to help us advance our goals. We can apply this whether we are working directly with someone on the same goal, or when we are lifting or edifying each other towards reaching higher and further. In the example of the body, just to crash with a knee strike, we are also using muscles in the back, arms, shoulders, legs, and abs, which come together and create a maximum impact. With your mind, you connect with others in mentor relationships, teams of people that specialize in areas in which you aren't as strong, and connections with like-minded people who are striving towards higher goals. The same approach you take to these activities will also generate positive energy and activities to enhance your future.

If you recall, I described one aspect of bursting as shielding with gross motor movement, such as 360 blocking while simultaneously attacking. This is important from a life aspect, too, because we hardly ever think to shield our minds before proceeding. Just as we would in a physical attack, sometimes we are better off defending our minds properly by having a better understanding of what we are dealing with before we jump in. Ask yourself, how often have you not bothered to ask proper questions when you take on a new venture, project, education, or goal, only to find yourself lacking in understanding, being overwhelmed, or succumbing to challenges that could have been resolved by proper thought processes?

Just as a burst is a moment of effective reaction that allows you to advance your goal in martial arts, a burst can also become an effective reaction to decisions you must make quickly. When you have to make a choice, certain knowledge may be revealed in your life, an opportunity is presented, and you must take immediate action and decide. In that instant, you must ask yourself, will I go for this opportunity or let it slide? If you go for it, the opportunity is created. If you don't, the opportunity may be taken away. In this type of situation, you take the information you have at the moment and make the best choice you can.

An example of a burst decision occurred when a friend of mine, who buys certain types of lien bonds, offered me the opportunity to purchase. From a burst standpoint, if I trust my friend's knowledge, it might be a good idea for me to go forward and buy several bonds. Another example was when a next-door neighbor, who is not an investor, offered me the chance to buy a property and asks me to pay a $5000 payment in good faith. I had to decide if it was worth the risk. I asked myself, Do I know enough to act on this opportunity? You have to be willing to take the effort and think on your feet to do a burst.

Be prepared to answer when faced with a burst decision.

Another example of a burst decision is an unexpected situation. A friend of mine went to a store to shop with a coworker. Someone who was outside of the store and looking for victims rushed up to the pair and demanded money for help. My friend reacted to the situation with a quick burst, blurting out, "We can't help you!" whereas her coworker said nothing. My friend and her coworker ran into the store. Thanks to her quick thinking, she avoided a potentially dangerous situation.

If you take a shortcut in your life and miss the mark, this is like using a fine technique in self-defense. It may result in ruin and failure. Remember, a fine technique or motor movement gives you a small chance of arresting or containing what is coming at you. But, because they are fine movements, your chance for missing is greater and may not contain or arrest the threat. For example, just as grabbing a wrist, threading a needle, or blocking with your palm are all fine motor movements from a physical standpoint, not doing proper research in your thought process could open you up to making a bad choice. Having an approach that shields you mentally from negative people and self-fear, on the other hand, will increase your chances for success. This is also true for general mental health. When our minds are not allowed to have a relaxed baseline, we will make decisions under stress which often throws us into turmoil. This negatively impacts our relationships, our work performance, and hurts people we care about. Everything from meditation to being in touch with how we respond to events in our lives is vital for balance and shielding.

There is a life lesson in bringing synergy to your life's goals. When we bring people around us who are smarter than we are and have wisdom to impart, they energize us. You will want to become a part of a team that is knowledgeable, a team that kickstarts you to move in the direction you want to head. Find out what your passion or goal is, and find a mentor who matches the field or area of your passion or goal. This mentor will help to keep you focused. What you gain from your experience and from the people with whom you choose to spend time is what makes you effective.

On the other hand, be wary of people offering help who are not the right mentor for you. Just like the person who thinks they can defend themselves but really is vulnerable, choosing the wrong mentor can create a false sense of protection for you.

Finally, do you have a responsibility to create a maximum impact in the life of others or only yourself? Consider your answer carefully. If you are reaching lots of people with what you do, your maximum impact reaches beyond your direct impact. It has a ripple effect. So, based on this knowledge, what will you choose to do?

FOLLOW YOUR PASSIONS, BUT BE STRATEGIC WITH YOUR CHOICES

Mike grew up being told, "you'll never be good at sports so just get good grades and stay out of trouble. You do that, and you'll do great in life." Mike bought into it. He produced high-performing grades and received awards for his efforts. His parents were proud. And when he was younger in school, he would always receive the citizenship awards because he was helpful, had a great attitude, and never got in trouble. As time went on, he watched his friends play sports and even cheered them on. He never got to participate on a team but played with the kids who were in sports. Anytime he approached his parents, they would always discourage him from pursuing sports.

As with many kids, when you start to grow up your voice gets smaller because you don't want to give the wrong answer or look stupid in the classroom or in front of your peers. This was even more important in high school due to peer pressure and ridicule. A couple of times when he spoke up to give the correct answers in school, it brought a backlash. So, he did not want anyone to know he got good grades.

He did well beyond high school and when he started working, a friend who knew he loved martial arts told him that she was taking a karate class. He went to the class and loved the atmosphere. He trained and even started going to competitions. He was visiting his parents during the holidays one year and had a heart-to-heart talk with them. He asked them why they never encouraged him to play sports as he had the same abilities as the guys that played. His father told him how he allowed his obsession with it to take him down the wrong path. His mother was always concerned he would be injured and felt academics would be more important.

Mike never really understood their reason, but he discovered how stifling this was to his development and his ability to challenge himself. He discovered he could do more. He could create a maximum impact by not being tethered to his past but releasing himself to his future. Note, he was not interested in just doing anything. As Lewis Carroll said, "If you don't know where you're going, any road will take you there."

To make a maximum impact Mike understood that he would have to be smart with his choices. He had to be strategic and he had to expand his knowledge to find the most efficient ways. Feeling many people, including his parents, were invested in him, Mike wanted to do the same for others. Even though he wasn't a top athlete in school, he became a motivational speaker and life coach because he wanted to create a maximum impact.

CHAPTER 3 - HOW CAN
I CREATE A MINIMAL
RISK FOR MYSELF?

In a self-defense situation, the last thing you want to do is put yourself in more danger while you are trying to protect yourself. The question you want to ask is, how can I create a minimal risk to myself? We will discuss methods and strategies to obtain that goal in this chapter.

Strategy number one in martial arts is to identify the threat. Without identifying the threat, you have no means to minimize the risk. You want to pick up on cues that will allow you to assess the possibilities. These cues can include a person's body posture, attitude, behavior, conversation, and positioning.

If the person you are facing is carrying themselves in a tense or swelling body posture, they may be upset about something that could cause them to strike out if provoked. The same logic follows in your daily life with someone exhibiting a strong attitude. Their excess energy should be a red flag to you that this person could be a threat.

For example, let's say it is a normal day, and you notice strange behavior such as someone following you or tracking your movements. This is your cue to pay attention. While this behavior does not necessarily mean anything is wrong, you don't want to be oblivious to it. Beware of people who seem to approach you for no reason to talk and encroach on your personal space. Immediately upon approach, reposition yourself and let them know you are uncomfortable through your body language, or verbally if necessary. When this type of situation occurs, you should also be scoping around you as this person may not be alone.

Conversation is twofold. If you notice the tone of a conversation becoming violent or threatening, you can de-escalate the tension with your tone and conversation. For example, let's say that you smile at someone. As you smile, their significant other walking beside them becomes offended and angrily asks, "Who are you smiling at?" Instead of snapping at them, you can choose to reply, "My apologies. I thought they were someone I knew. I meant no disrespect. Can I buy you a beer (if at a bar or restaurant)?" De-escalation is better than a confrontation.

Be prepared to de-escalate a tense situation.

If a stranger is engaging you in conversation, be aware of your position to them, and always ensure you are able to see around you. Pay attention to your gut feelings, too. If something doesn't feel right, trust that reaction, as it usually is correct. If you have that strange feeling, immediately create some space for yourself. You can say, "Sir, I don't feel comfortable with you being this close to me."

Often a conversation with a stranger is not dangerous, and I am not promoting that you be on your guard all the time. When it comes to conversations with a stranger, obviously there is a spectrum. The types of conversations can range from someone asking, "Do you know what time it is" and "Can you point me in the right direction," to someone being overly aggressive in engaging with you and trying to control you and your movement. The manner of conversation can move to be beyond acceptable, from pressuring you with kindness all the way to being belligerent and directing you to do something. Consider the possibility that the person confronting you may be mentally ill. In this case, your intent should change as your best choice may be to avoid agitating the person. No matter what the situation is, your goal at all times is to place yourself in a position where the other person won't hurt you.

You always want to position yourself so that you can observe most of the area around you. You can achieve this by standing with your feet at a 45-degree angle. Standing this way will allow you to see more area because your body will also be angled. If you pay attention, often you can observe members of law enforcement standing with their feet at a 45-degree angle.

Standing at a 45 degree angle.

Standing at this angle allows you to move to a stable position as well as providing you with the ability to run if you need to. But if you are flat-footed while facing the person, be aware that someone can come up from behind you. In this situation, you could be pushed down. You will have to alter your body position before moving away from your aggressor. Like a tango or a waltz, you can't position yourself without footwork. In Krav Maga, there is a move you can do when someone tries to hold a knife to your throat. When it comes to your stance, if you pay attention to your feet and where you are in reference to objects, obstacles, and people, you can maneuver to positions that you can either evade or defend from.

Balance is crucial with positioning, too. Be careful and use stances for mobility and stability. The lower your body is set, the more stable you are. The higher your body is set, the more mobile you are.

I recommend you keep your "red alert on safety." When you put a gun on safety, it means you place it in a position where the trigger will not activate. I use this expression to describe the goal to live as safely as possible but to continue to enjoy your daily activities, and not to put yourself in a metaphorical box. If you ever had the responsibility to watch or care for a child, pet, or parent, you made yourself aware of their activities and acted accordingly when needed. Your awareness was higher while you were still able to complete or enjoy your activity, even with your additional responsibility. While you don't lower your mental guard altogether, you do want to enable yourself to bring up your physical guard immediately when needed. You are aware of potential "red alert" scenarios, but you keep your "safety" on, meaning that you don't overreact.

Now let's look at physical methods and strategies for creating minimal risk.

If a person has caught you off guard, you should immediately attempt to shield yourself versus trying to block or strike because you are not prepared to do so from a position of stability. Shielding consists of covering the area that is being attacked. By shielding yourself or covering yourself, it also gives you an extra second of time to decide your next move. In most cases, it will be your head that is under attack. One way you can shield yourself is to cover both sides of your head with your hands and arms. There are also elbow techniques that can be used in this position. In this case, you use your elbows not to stay covered, but to be able to move when caught off-guard.

Using your elbows as a shield to block strikes. This is called the RHINO position.

To avoid or limit an attack, sometimes you are best served using angling because the person will have to change their direction to pursue you. In these situations, I recommend that you angle your body instead of standing to face your attacker directly. By moving at an angle, you can run past the person, block them from coming back at you, or work your way to their back through blocking and striking. Placing yourself at this angle also gives you a better opportunity to use chokes and holds. But at other times, by moving straight ahead when the opportunity presents itself, you can neutralize an attack quickly.

Lastly, let's discuss blocking. As we touched on in the previous chapter, blocking with gross or larger motor movements is better than blocking with fine motor movement. Which is easier to use to hit a fly: your bare hand or a fly swatter? The fly swatter has a larger surface area and therefore provides a wider contact area than your hand, even when moving faster.

Similarly, if you have ever tried to catch either a full-speed punch or a fly, you know that it is not easy to do. Therefore, this activity doesn't minimize your risk. In systems like Krav Maga, 360° blocking allows you a better chance to avoid and dissipate the strike.

Everything we have just discussed minimizes your risk of being injured in a physical confrontation. But what are you doing to minimize mental risks in your life? Are you paying attention to the conversations you are having with others? Are you aware of the impact of what you say is having on the other person? If not, you are not protecting your mind.

How often do you limit interactions with negative people or people who have a bad attitude? Each time you allow yourself exposure to these types of people, you are not protecting yourself.

When was the last time you decided to limit your time with entertainment or social media? If you spend unlimited time on these pastimes, you are not protecting yourself because you are allowing yourself to drift mentally by living through the activities of others. You may also be basing your current situation on what you perceive as a better life as portrayed on social media which in fact may be false. When you allow yourself to compare your real life to these one-dimensional portrayals of life, you often don't see yourself for the value you actually have. Frequently people present themselves on social media in a way that has nothing to do with their actual lives or their problems.

Are you ignoring events around you when you are on your phone or checking out social media?

If we reduce our intake of entertainment or social media and instead choose meditation, prayer, mindfulness, and quiet time, we can make our senses keener for what's going on around us. Only when we quiet our minds can we truly relax.

We place alarm systems on our homes and cars and establish parental controls for our children, but we don't spend adequate time protecting our minds through what we feed our brains and our spirit. We allow ourselves to be led by the masses. When we do this, we endanger our ability to learn, to achieve higher goals, and to maximize the blessing that is our life.

WATCH FOR RED FLAGS, SET BOUNDARIES, AND PROTECT YOUR HEART

Steve was a people pleaser who always gave people many chances. He wanted to feel needed, appreciated, and worthy. With family and love relationships, he would let people walk all over him. He would never limit access to his heart and feelings, while at the same time he ignored red flags. Making excuses for them, he would say "that's just how they are," "they can change," "they've been through a lot," and many more. It truly impacted him when he felt people weren't happy with him. And somehow, that was a major part of his existence. Last but not least, he had a complex about being worthy to be part of the team, organization, or social gathering. In relationships, he was verbally abused and talked down to by family who was dismissive of his opinions and would bulldoze his ideas as trivial. Meanwhile, in love relationships, he was a doormat. He would go to great lengths to meet the needs of the other person and their desires but in return, his needs and desires were not even considered.

He trained as a gymnast and accepted his coach's opinion of him as if this coach was a god. He took medications, which masked the pain of injuries. He never even shared this with his coach because he did not want to be seen as weak.

Now as you look at this situation, you may think, "wow, this guy is fit, possibly good-looking, and liked by everyone"... and you would be right. But because he didn't create a minimal risk to himself by putting the proper, healthy relationship boundaries in place, he did not enjoy life. He lived with anxiety and a word from one person could destroy him emotionally for the day (without anyone even knowing it, because he never expressed it). Now do not get it wrong, he experienced happy moments in his life, but generally, he wasn't happy or truly enjoying life or his potential because he wasn't protecting it.

One day Steve was speaking with Ally, a fellow gymnast from another organization he had known for years and always looked forward to connecting with. They were having coffee and checking in on how life was going for each of them. Steve finally broke down and shared how the anxiety he was experiencing. He explained that the relationship with his coach was dampening his spirit and he did not know what direction to go in. Ally was shocked because she saw Steve as having high energy, always raising the spirit of everyone in his presence, and an example of strength and determination. She had seen Steve stand up for others and the issues he believed in. To find out that someone was walking all over him, impacting his life to this extent, just did not click.

She asked him how he could allow people to manipulate and control such a strong component of his life, especially because he was such a leader in everything he did.He had to stop and say to himself, "she is right." He had led himself and others to so many achievements. He had mentored people to find their potential and he loved the people in his life relentlessly. He asked himself where he went wrong. Then he started to coach himself. He had to review all the areas of his life where he went down the wrong path to end up where he was now. He found that it came down to three things: red flags, boundaries, and protecting his heart from manipulation.

Red flags were something that he ignored often as he typically put himself on the back burner. In his family, he found himself being used for financial support yet ignored in decision making whether it was his spouse or the family he grew up with. He finally stood up and told them of the value he placed on their lives and that he had value himself. He would no longer be unheard. They would have to respect his boundaries, thoughts on issues, and ideas for the future. He had to act on all the red flags he saw so he could create a minimal risk to his life. By the proper response, he could evade, avoid, and deal with red flags that crossed his path.

Boundaries were something he did not have. People had too much access to him and he had made himself available to them 24/7. Because he did this, he worked harder to maintain productivity in his life. He could see that he brought all of this on himself. He started to set boundaries to complete tasks, to not be engaged in manipulation, and to get his life back. He even stepped away from his coach and started working with another organization which allowed him to soar in accomplishments. He has also helped others meet their accomplishments.

Protecting his heart from boundaries was challenging because he appreciated relationships, but he found that this was a weak area that he could no longer allow being manipulated and therefore attacked. Without recognizing red flags to avoid, evade, or neutral manipulation, he would be entangled making it harder to get out of. He also realized that just because he forgave people, he did not have to let them back in a position to use him again. He now shares his experiences with others so they can gain control of their lives by creating a minimal risk to themselves.

What areas of your life do you need to create a minimal risk to yourself?

CHAPTER 4 - WHAT IS OODA LOOP AND HOW CAN I USE IT?

The OODA Loop is a process cycle that was developed by Air Force Lieutenant John Boyd. Created and used for operational campaigns in the military, the acronym OODA stands for **Observe, Orient, Decide,** and **Act**. It is referred to as a loop because it is a continuous process.

The first letter is O, for **Observe**. By observing your environment, you increase the likelihood of seeing potential threats before they occur. This is important because when you detect them ahead of time, you can avoid these threats. Every day, people get into situations they never saw coming in which they were caught off guard. Sometimes we are preoccupied or we are oblivious because we are lulled into a false sense of security. When we are observant, we can not only perceive potential threats and avoid them, but we can also enjoy life more because we are aware of our surroundings and their opportunities.

An example of this is observing your surroundings when you visit a new city and go for a walk. By paying attention to the people and buildings around you, you can tell if you need to move away from your current position or maintain your position for safety. And you can also enjoy seeing new sights. You will want to be observant if someone comes running up to you suddenly, but you also want to enjoy your surroundings as well.

Always observe your surroundings.

Now that you have observed your surroundings, you must **Orient** yourself to the things in it, which is the second letter O. In a threatening situation, you may need to hide or move to safety. If you can't find a place to move away or hide, you may have to fight. This is where your resourcefulness and mindset come into play. If you have not developed skills to defend yourself, look for improvised weapons such as keys, utensils, pens, and items to throw. Or look for large objects to help you to barricade yourself. By applying some of the earlier principles we discussed and by obtaining training in practical self-defense, you will increase your chances of survival if you have to fight. Please consider learning skills and taking training, such as Krav Maga, as a necessity in case you are forced to defend yourself physically. But, as you can see, no matter what your existing skill level is, you have the ability to orient yourself before taking action.

Let's discuss the next step in the OODA Loop, the letter D for **Decide**. Deciding what you will do is a 'make it or break it' moment in the OODA Loop process. When you observe your situation and orient yourself, you can gather information from your external environment and your internal environment to decide what to do next.

Within the external environment, you can observe potential obstacles that could prevent you from escaping, items within your environment you can use to defend yourself, and you can start assessing what you have the ability to do. You can ask questions, such as: Where is the door? Could you use that item as a weapon? Do you have a clear exit available to you? Do I have the skills to take on this opponent? Am I feeling strong enough to take action? What am I willing to do? By observing yourself, you can assess the skills you have, what your physical limitations may be in this situation, and what you are mentally prepared to do.

Using both your external and internal environment, you have to make a decision or it could cost you your life. Once you have decided upon and executed an action, you must follow it all the way through. Why? It is because you have no choice except to follow your action through if you are going to make it home. While choosing a decision is key to making it home in a situation where we are physically confronted, too often we forget how necessary these decisions are to everyday life decisions, too. Every time you make an assessment before you act, you give yourself time to think about what the repercussions could be. You may be saying to yourself, "I already make hundreds of decisions a day." Yes, all of us have to make many decisions. What I want you to consider are the decisions you don't make that can lead you to live an average life or mediocre life.

What do I mean by this? An example of these decisions is when we choose not to take care of ourselves through exercise, sleep, and personal enrichment to grow. When we avoid making healthy choices, we are making choices that damage our lives. How often have you told a child, someone you mentor or someone for whom you care, to take their medicine? We do this because the individual needs their medicine to be well, and because we care for and love them, we remind them to take it. Too often we don't show the same love to ourselves, however, and this is damaging. It impacts our ability to be better for ourselves and to show up for the people in our lives who rely on us.

I want you to ask yourself, "Am I getting the physical activity I need to improve my health? Am I working on proper sleep patterns that allow my body to rest and recover, which makes me more productive? Am I reading, learning, and participating in furthering my education of my mind and life?" As you can see, each of these questions prompt you to reach for something better.

People who take care of themselves don't do what is

comfortable or stay in the status quo. They know they have a responsibility first to themselves, and then to those they love, to make choices that allow them to reach their full potential. And as we all know, it is not easy to change, but it is necessary. Once you make that decision, you can only make it happen through action.

In the OODA Loop acronym, the letter A stands for **Act**. During this step, everything goes into motion. It is the point when you make the decision and act to defend yourself or escape, depending on your options and strategies. If you choose to escape, you should have already envisioned how that option will play out by orienting yourself to your environment. By getting the "lay of the land," you may find it is prudent to escape. So, you move to your escape route and evade the scene, knowing you will not stop moving away until it is safe to do so.

When you decide to defend yourself, you must effectively do so with everything you have. As we stated earlier, you must drive forward and continue to fight until it is safe to leave. With proper training, you can fight in this manner by creating a massive impact but with minimal risk to yourself. Why is this important? When you don't bring a massive impact, you may be overwhelmed by retaliation.

In terms of our daily lives, how often do we actively decide to make a massive impact? How often do we just settle or make a partial effort? And how often do we resign to defeat? Too often we really want to pursue something in our lives but we settle for not doing it whenever we meet obstacles and adversity. Examples can include wanting to attend college but never make the attempt, or desiring a new career but allowing fear to change your mind. What is it about wanting to quit when things get challenging and hard? Why do we try to make ourselves feel better about giving up, and even go so far as justifying that it wasn't worth pursuing, only to reflect on what could have been? We even let friends, family, and colleagues convince us that we are better off or it will not be worth all we will be going through to achieve our goal.

A real-life example of meeting adversity. Here is my sister receiving her Ph.D. in leadership.

If you think about it, from a self-defense standpoint, your life is on the line, so what will you do to save it? From a successful life standpoint, your life is also on the line, because we only get one shot in our life journey. So what will you do to save yours?

ARE YOU PAYING ATTENTION?

Lee and Alan worked for the same company. They eventually worked their way into management. Proving themselves to be high performers, Lee and Alan helped hire new employees, develop teams, and work on projects that took the company higher. Now, while Alan always kept his ear to the ground, Lee only paid attention to what he was responsible for in his position. Besides, Lee had various interests outside of the company. As time went on, Alan saw the changes in direction that the company was going. In 2008, he saw that the company was scaling back. Lee kept with what he was doing and didn't pay attention to the impact it would have. He felt it would work out.

While Alan paid attention to the results and trends, he requested to step down from his management position to become a specialist instead. Lee saw managers being let go above him and employees being let go below him but just kept working, because he thought it would all work out.

Well, after working on a community project for the company, Alan returned to the office and received a call from human resources. Upon his arrival to human resources, he found that his position was being downsized. When he asked if he could step down, he was told there had only been two positions that could have been filled. Guess what, one of them had been filled by Lee. Lee recognized the business environment he was working in, oriented himself to all the moving parts, then decided what he could do, and acted on it. He knew due to his track record, he could work his way back into management once things were better. But in 2008, Lee knew he had to survive the financial storm. Lee is now a director with the company, while Alan is no longer in the industry at all.

Where have you failed to use an OODA loop in your personal or professional life? Did it cost you? Or did you observe the environment, orient yourself to flags, obstacles, activities, and trends that allowed you to make decisions to come out on top and act?

CHAPTER 5 - WHAT IS KADIMA AND HOW CAN I USE IT TO BE SUCCESSFUL IN ATTACKS?

'Kadima' is a Hebrew word which has several synonyms: forward, onward, hurry up, and quickly. In Israeli Krav Maga, Kadima means you drive forward to complete the goal of neutralizing an attack. As we discussed in previous chapters, you must be explosive in your action and sure in your intention. This is vital because it can be the difference in whether you survive or not.

Kadima speaks to the D in the OODA loop, **Decide**. After you have observed your environment, and have oriented yourself to what is in your environment, then you have to decide what you can do and how you can be successful. Once you make this decision, you must commit to moving forward once you begin to move.

Have you seen a deer turn tail and run away when confronted? Just like a deer, if I respond immediately, I may be able to move off and run before an attack occurs. But if I run, I cannot then hesitate, and I must have a plan of where I am going in order to maintain my safety.

Use the mindset of Kadima to move forward to neutralize an attack.

If you are in a scenario in which you can't run, you may have to defend yourself with what you have around you or use a skill set in which you have trained. But, here is what's vital. **If you choose to fight, you have to continue until it is safe to leave.**

Too often people have thought, "If I can just get that one good blow or that strike to the groin, then I can run away." The reality is if you take that action, you elevate the level of danger in the situation. After you strike, you may hurt the attacker, but they may not be down and unable to fight. The attacker may be on drugs and not feel the effects of your "one-shot" self-defense response. If you try to run, they may grab you or catch you. However, if you continue to attack, deciding to keep your stance and not run, you have created the opportunity to disable, destabilize, and injure your attacker so they cannot follow you or continue to attack you. You are turning the tables on them and making them wish they had chosen to attack someone else. Let's touch on that for a minute.

People only attack someone if they think they are going to win. They don't choose the strongest and biggest person to assault. They don't choose the person they think will give them the best fight. And they certainly don't choose someone that carries themselves as if they are skilled. What they want is someone who is a victim, who is going to give the least amount of fight so they can get away quickly from the situation when they are done. The attacker first scopes out and becomes aware of their surroundings, and then they choose someone who is not paying attention. Before they attack, they have planned and know their next move: they are going to drag you off into the woods or behind a building, alley, or into a vehicle. As warriors, it's important for us to have a plan before anything starts, too.

Sun Tzu stated in his book, *The Art of War,* that "Every battle is won or lost before it's ever fought." Similarly, we must have a plan. And a major part of that plan has to be Kadima. Why? By having the mindset of driving forward until the battle is won, you commit to your action. Without that outlook, you may freeze, second guess yourself, fall into a victim mindset or fail to act. By training to have a Kadima mindset, you know that no matter what, you have to keep moving forward.

Using a Kadima mindset in these instances means you are also using a warrior mindset. A Special Forces operator told me he was called a killer after returning from a war. The operator told the person that he absolutely wasn't a killer, as he always operated from a warrior mindset. He went on to explain that a killer wants to fight and win, but a warrior wants to protect themselves and those they are defending. So, ask yourself, if you were in a dangerous situation, who would you be willing to survive for?? Would it be your family and friends? Who and what would be so important to you that you must get home to them? Any of us can use this warrior mindset and use Kadima to survive an attack.

In fact, many men and women have survived incredible odds throughout time with this mentality. They may or may not have called it Kadima, but it was this principle that pulled them through. We have all heard stories of animal attacks on land and in the water in which people found a way to survive. People have also survived being stranded in various environments on the planet. There is something in all of us that wants to survive. But I want to encourage you to not just survive, but survive well! I encourage you to live your full life and champion your purpose.

Some of us lose this ability within us to survive, however. Some aren't willing to fight for their lives. They just settle for what is, like everyone else. The longer they live, the more they let life beat them down, just succumbing to the fight and giving up. If you think like this, you have just stamped 'victim' on your head. You have just yielded your life.

Maybe you didn't win the game as a child but you received a participation trophy. Did you then choose to only compete in events where you knew you would be rewarded, even if you weren't the best? You may win at something you do well, but how often do you challenge yourself to try something you don't do as well? You may be losing an opportunity to not just live but thrive.

If you ask a question in a first- or second-grade classroom, all of their hands go up. However, if you ask kids in a high school class a question, their hands come up slowly. Why is that? As we grow older, we have become conditioned not to be wrong or appear to be wrong. Taking a chance with the possibility that you could be wrong is to be avoided, and as a result, we think we look better if no one knows that we don't know. Hmm, what does that sound like, maybe an adult in corporate life? Even people who may be seen as superior athletes and fighters, sometimes even geniuses, have areas of their lives that they avoid in order to feel better about themselves. If we don't challenge ourselves or have the courage to fail in small ways, we are giving up. And giving up goes against the Kadima mindset.

If you have ever done any fight training, you know at some point you will get hit. This can feel intimidating at first. The more you practice, however, the more you become used to it, so getting hit doesn't feel as daunting anymore. You keep practicing to develop the skills to navigate the fight, so you are not only defending yourself but becoming effective at countering an attack. You become able to effectively attack for yourself. If you accomplished this type of training and practice through time in one area of your life, why isn't this reflected in other areas of your life?

This is where embracing the concept of Kadima is important, and we can use it in order to rediscover ourselves. In fact, we can fight through anything that is important to us. In all areas of your life, relationships, careers, goals, entrepreneurship, or survival, please don't settle. Vow to live your life to the fullest.

We can use Kadima in all aspects of our lives. In business, using this mindset to be proactive with clients is a smart strategy.

Kadima doesn't mean quit, give up, give in or procrastinate. We started this chapter understanding how we need the Kadima mindset to help us survive and attack, so we can fight on so we can ultimately return home. But as I mentioned before, we can't get home unless we are willing to continue to fight until the battle is over.

Why not live every day with a warrior mindset to push forward? Why do we give up when obstacles confront us? Why not search for the ability within us to make the changes and meet the challenges that will allow us to live to the fullest? When we lose sight of our Kadima mindset, that drive, that all-out effort that will bring us victory, we settle for less. I challenge you: Why don't you go all out to change your life? Is it the challenge? Is it the obstacles? Is it because you are worried about what someone may say? Is it the chance that you might fail?

Imagine what your life would look like if you decided to make choices that would propel you forward. What if you met obstacles that enabled you to grow and tackled higher obstacles that will make you excel? Keep in mind that people can't add to you or take away from you. Only you can! Failures have built empires through time, as people revisit, revise, and redo to create success. When will you start yours?

We can die a death of a thousand cuts due to the little decisions we make on a daily basis that end up wounding us deeply in the long run. A little compromise here and there can add up to an entire life built around resistance. But if we have a code that we live by, a mantra, or a standard, then we can build systems of behavior around that standard that will allow us to utilize Kadima to discontinue the wrong decisions and drive us forward to the right decisions. Remember, there are as many variables that impact wrong decisions as there are right ones. We just have to make sure we are moving forward by the standard and system we choose to allow us to win.

Too often in life, we allow setbacks, obstacles, and emotions to keep us from the finish line. I challenge you to be a warrior and fight forward, fail forward, and win forward for what is important to you.

KEEP MOVING FORWARD

James was always seen as having high potential in life. He excelled in school, had a flair for construction even as a child, and wanted to become an architect. Soon after he graduated from high school, he lost his parents in a car accident. Because there were no relatives to speak of, he took custody of his brother who was nonverbal and autistic. In the past, he didn't have to worry about caring for his brother because his parents were always there. He knew his brother was in good hands, so he continued to look towards the future. But now, he felt an obligation to take care of the brother he loved. He worked and struggled to make ends meet for them because his parents didn't have adequate life insurance. He was fortunate that he had started working in high school. The manager of the business where he worked was understanding and respected his efforts, but it didn't make it any less challenging.

James still had the dream of becoming an architect. He read books, watched videos, and over time he connected to a couple of people that were doing what he wanted to do. So, he stayed in the fight.

When it came to his brother, he found out which services were publicly available to him. He also connected with nonprofit organizations that were both resources and support groups. Even though he had dreams of what he wanted, he also wanted his brother to have the best quality of life available. He always said, "family first."

Later, he fell in love and was eventually married. Unfortunately, it didn't last because his situation with caring for his brother hadn't changed. She found it was more than she could bear. He was heartbroken but never gave up. James believed in love and knew there was someone out there for him. It was years before he had a viable relationship again. He found himself falling into depression over his situation, but he surrounded himself with people that were in the fight as well. His autism family support groups were invaluable during these times and kept him moving forward. He took courses in architecture. After he completed his schooling, the architects he networked with eventually helped him land a job within their firm.

He had always been responsible with his finances but now he had adequate funds to hire someone full-time to care for his brother. Gina was an excellent caregiver for his brother and he never saw his brother respond to anyone the way he reacted to her. After Gina had been with them for over a year, he started to see her for all that she was. The same feelings happened for her but they didn't act on it because they had a professional relationship. They both wanted what was best for the brother. When his brother passed away two years later due to other health issues, Gina and James looked to each other for support. They would talk on the phone and reminisce about the brother. They would meet for coffee.

Then after a couple of months of dating, they fell in love and eventually got married. They have been together ever since and have two beautiful children. He would say he never stopped believing in love and kept moving forward until he found it.

With all of his struggles, adversity, and losses, James never had a bad attitude or allowed himself to have a "Woe is me" outlook on life. He was young and could have allowed his brother to be a ward of the state or abandoned him. He could have said, "forget my dreams of love and being an architect." Or he could have thought, "why bother, I'll never get there...The mountain is too high to climb and I have too many obstacles in my way." He could have settled for what is and had been thankful but that's not what he did.

He lived out the concept of Kadima by not just having the will to survive and move forward, but by being intentional about his goals and not second-guessing himself. As the old saying goes, "it's not the dog in the fight, but the fight in the dog." He found a large enough why and fought for it every step of the way. To see him today, you would never know what he went through to get there. I have heard many celebrities, athletes, and leaders break it down this way: You see the glory of what has been accomplished but you don't know the story of how the person got there.

Just like a self-defense situation, decide that you will move forward and survive whatever comes your way because you are here for a purpose.

CHAPTER 6 - WHAT DOES THE GRAY MAN HAVE TO DO WITH MY ABILITY TO DEFEND MYSELF?

Being the center of attention can be a plus, but did you realize it can also put you into a dangerous situation? If you dress in bright colors, give a lot of eye contact, have a strong demeanor, wear an intense perfume or cologne, or speak loudly, you are more likely to draw notice to yourself. Being the Gray Man is the opposite of these actions. The Gray Man is a concept taught in martial arts that allows you to evade a confrontation or crisis by not drawing attention to yourself and enabling you to quietly remove yourself from a situation.

When you are in public, if you have not observed your surroundings (remember, the first letter O in OODA loop) and are startled, you may scream. Suddenly because you have made a loud noise, all eyes are on you. However, if you were aware of how many people were within earshot of you, your mindset could prepare you, and you may not be startled at all. Therefore, you would be able to act calmly and not bring attention to yourself.

The Gray Man concept is about being able to blend into your environment. By taking this action, you reduce your likelihood of being a target. By not provoking or inducing a response from the people around you, it gives you the best opportunity to escape if the situation escalates. Have you ever needed to leave a meeting or a party but didn't want to draw attention to yourself while leaving? You may have waited until everyone was engaged by some conversation or other stimulus to make your exit. This is a Gray Man activity.

Being the Gray Man means blending into the crowd.

What is the value in acting as the Gray Man? In self-defense, if you are not seen or noticed, you aren't perceived as a threat and may be able to avoid a crisis. The question is, how does this apply to the rest of your life? Ask yourself, how often are you drawing people into your life you should avoid because of how you are perceived by others?

We can't just let anyone and everyone into our space or our lives. But too often we let strangers, overbearing coworkers, and even family members have way more time, space, and energy in our lives than they should. These people have negative energy or may have ideas that do not support our values or goals. It is too easy to fall into the trap of letting in people who don't add value to your life, allowing them to drain your energy.

What can you do about it? Use the same skills you would use in self-defense to defend your life! I challenge you to develop a game plan to keep away from these people.

First and foremost, observe people's behavior and demeanor. Are they always acting in a negative way? Are they always complaining? Do they always talk about, and in fact invite, drama or conflict in their lives? Do they interact with you as a peer, or do they seek you out to be their personal sounding board without listening to you? Do they try to pull you into their drama? Do they feel they can encroach on your time, no matter what you are doing?

Just as you blend to avoid attention in the crowd by employing the methods of being the Gray Man, you can deflect their negativity by showing disinterest in their conversation. These people want you to get riled up. They will try to stir you up by getting you involved. But, if you are respectfully disinterested, these "energy vampires" will approach you less and less. This works the same with other toxic people. When you give people the energy they are looking for, they will continue coming to you. If you remove your energy from them, they will move on and seek others.

Avoid people who don't support you or act negatively.

Add boundaries to your interactions with people in your life. When you find your circle of mentors as we discussed in Chapter 2, the people who build you up and give you more energy and support your vision, welcome them in. These people are worthy to have access. Limit access to those who are not deserving of your full energy and attention. Having healthy boundaries is essential.

WATCH, WAIT, AND KNOW WHEN TO ACT

Have you ever heard the saying, "watch the quiet ones"? That was what saved Brian's life. He never wanted to bring attention to himself but he was always watching what was going on around him. He may have even let you know what was going on. Whether it was a couple arguing or someone wearing something outlandish, he would look at you to gain your attention, whisper in your ear, or even text you during an outing to point them out.

One weekend, he and some friends were at a food court when he noticed a group of guys come in together then disburse around the area. He could see they were looking around and watching the perimeter. He felt this couldn't be good and decided to watch the one closest to him who was facing the hall heading toward the bathrooms. It seemed the guys closest to the bathroom were watching the doors carefully. He whispered to his friends that something was up and then they individually looked for an opportunity to slip past the guy facing the hall for the bathroom. After all of them had gotten into the hall and close to the bathroom, they heard the guys shouting. Brian and his friends kept going down the hall until they found an outdoor exit and left the mall. Once outside, one friend called the police while another called the mall office to alert security. Brian and his friends didn't know what happened afterwards but they knew they escaped a potentially dangerous situation.

By not pulling attention to themselves and getting out of harm's way, they were able to save themselves and others when the police moved in.

Eunice, an analyst with her company, was very observant. During meetings, she didn't contribute much from a speaking standpoint. However, there were several people who lived to make a point and show how intelligent they were. Meanwhile, Eunice maintained her observation of people and looked for which talents, skills, and abilities others brought to the table. She found that Tom was good at speaking, while Jesse was good with numbers, and Camille was good with presentations and research.

Eunice had an idea that she felt would raise the company's brand. She pulled Tom, Camille, and Jesse together to work their part and gain their buy-in. Together, they created a very professional and thorough presentation. The board agreed it would be monumental. After the presentation, Eunice did the closing and Q&A session. Everyone in the company was mystified and wondered how she could pull something like that together. As a result, she became the project manager and everyone wanted her for their projects. She didn't stay in the shadows to just blend in with her colleagues. Instead, Eunice watched. Not only did she know what she brought to the table, but what others brought as well. It paid off for her to be the gray man in her environment by watching and waiting to act.

CHAPTER 7 - WHAT DOES "BEING LIKE WATER" MEAN?

Bruce Lee, the Hong Kong-American actor, director, martial artist, martial arts instructor, and philosopher, famously shared during an interview what it means to "be the nature of water." He said, "Empty your mind, be formless, shapeless. You put water in a cup, it becomes the cup. Be water, my friend." He felt his martial art expression, Jeet Kune Do, which means "way of the intercepting fist," was not about form, but instead was about being adaptable. Allow me to explain.

Bruce Lee objected to forms of martial arts he felt were too formalized in stances and fixed positions, as he believed they did not allow for means of self-expression. For many years martial art forms have depended on certain standard stances. Lee found when he would study the form of these stances, he could analyze them and beat his opponent. Instead of relying on predictable moves, he championed a more dynamic and less patterned way of moving.

When you are in a fight, if you're only used to acting from a standpoint of stability, that's okay. From a stable position, it is easier to adapt to your opponent's moves because the pressure is not as high. But what happens if you are under attack by someone moving towards you? That's a violent, high-pressure situation. Under threat, it is harder to maneuver, as your proficiency level is lowered. If all you have studied are standard stances, and someone rushes towards you, you may have used your one move, and now, out of moves, you are in trouble.

Being attacked while standing still versus being attacked while in motion.

You can change this by learning to adapt. By being the nature of water, you're flowing with what's going on. It is a different mindset because you start operating from a concept, not a technique. From a self-defense standpoint, if you are caught up in a technique approach, that means you have only learned to copy and emulate that technique. If you try to use that technique and fail, it will be harder to adapt.

If I teach you to operate from a concept, however, you now have thousands of options. When you learn a concept, you have learned to take a repeatable maneuver and mix it up depending on the situation you are facing. You have learned a skill rather than a single move.

Another martial arts concept that illustrates being like water is displacing energy versus fighting straight on. If you hold out your fist and someone pushes against it, it is hard to move. Since all of your opponent's energy is exerted against your fist, you are resisting force with force, which is hard to deflect. But by displacing a strike instead of thrusting out your fist, the other person doesn't block the full impact of your energy and it allows you to be mobile for a continuous response.

Choose how to block a strike.

In self-defense, if I influence you by making you think about what I can do to you, you may cower instead of thinking about what you can do. At that point, I have a knowledge base from which I can operate. In this situation, to be like water, I challenge my students to be clear on how things work together. Which moves will allow them to be more flexible during an attack? Water flows and molds but doesn't disrupt. It is so powerful that it can break things and destroy, but it can also shape a new path like a river.

There are a number of ways we can apply this philosophy to our daily decisions and interactions in order to not just survive but thrive. One way we can be like water in our daily lives is through communication. Communication has properties like water. Two people can be in the same current, or one person can stop or dam up the communication. If you are open to receive a message, you will hear it.

 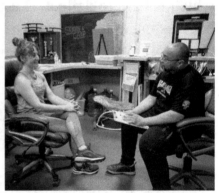

Strive to have good communication.

Water has many characteristics. In warm conditions, water flows. In freezing weather, water becomes ice, a solid form. Similarly, we have varied talents and can adapt to multiple situations. Many times, we adopt this philosophy of 'I can only do one thing' while we are growing up. If we show an aptitude for math, for example, others may see us and label us as a math whiz. Also, we might only consider one occupation based on our family history. For example, we might say to ourselves, "My father was a police officer so I should be a police officer." But what if there are other options available to us? Are we open to them?

If we open our minds and accept there are new possibilities, we can create a new 'us.' As a result, we become stronger than we were before. Adaptability enables us to discover who we can truly be.

It's that type of adaptability, being changeable like water, that allows us to excel not only in self-defense but also in our business and our personal life. If you simply adopt the framework of someone else, you are just duplicating them. While it is helpful to adopt smart practices in your business, it is important to be flexible, open to change, and tailor practices to suit who you are.

Another way we can be adaptable is through examining our processes. For example, technology changes constantly. If you were to decide that you never wanted to update your technology, you would soon find yourself unable to do business and communicate.

Another way in which we can be like water is in our approach to making money. Robert Kiyosaki, the American businessman and author of *Rich Dad Poor Dad,* has demonstrated this creativity throughout his life and career. He started two companies that eventually became bankrupt. He didn't let that stop him, however. He started a third, an educational company, that he sold before writing his first book which launched his successful Rich Dad and Cashflow brands. He wanted to share with people how to succeed in real estate since that was the main source of his success. An interesting fact is that the book "Rich

Dad Poor Dad" was written to promote a board game that Kiyosaki developed. People responded so positively to his book that it became a phenomenon, eclipsing the game. He changed his focus from promoting the game to promoting his book instead.

Like water, Robert's path was diverted numerous times. He learned from his best friend's dad that it is necessary to grow and learn from your mistakes in order to succeed. He could have given up at that point and accepted defeat. Instead, he took the lessons learned and created new companies that were successful. Another way to put this is, "If opportunity doesn't knock, build a door."

Just as water can cut a path through rock over a length of time, so too can we carve the path to our best lives over a number of years. Just as the water clears debris that was not needed, so too can we identify and utilize the things we need and get rid of what we don't.

Also, understanding the nature of water itself can assist us. If you have ever been to the Roanoke Sound in the Outer Banks, you know it divides the central Outer Banks from Roanoke Island. As a result, the water is very calm. Usually, the water is so still that you can see to the bottom and the water looks like glass. However, if you walk through or disturb the floor of this same water, it quickly becomes murky.

How many times in your life have you longed for clarity, but because you keep moving and never stop to rest, everything still appears cloudy to you? Sometimes we have to separate ourselves from other people to find the calm in ourselves. Our lives are like this, too. If you keep stirring things up, your path in life will be murky. If you let things filter or settle, however, you can see more clearly.

You need to still the mud. Sometimes you might have to run things through a screen to get impurities out, like toxic people. And if you aren't willing to do the screening, well, you get the mud.

When you become like water and still yourself to gain clarity, you will discover the role you play. By doing this you are using mindfulness. This is very powerful because with mindfulness, you choose whether your vision of your world is clear or murky. We all have to coexist in the world, and therefore we have to be able to understand who we are so we can respond to the world.

Currently, the "Us vs. Them" mindset is prevalent in the United States. It is easy to get stirred up when people are taking sides and arguing, with a hasty determination that "we are right and you are wrong." The danger of this mindset is you can become so consumed with your ideas that you stop considering the ideas of others. Like blocked water, you dam up. Water that cannot flow becomes stagnant, and so too can the minds of people who stop allowing new ideas in.

This type of thinking has existed for thousands of years. An example is in the Bible, where the apostle Paul writes to the Church Laodicea. He advises the parishioners that their mindset is faulty. The people of the church have been thinking that in order to do business you had to do what other people are doing, even if their actions were wrong. They were telling themselves, "I'm making money so I will look away." Paul tells them you have to look at who you are serving.

The best mindset is to be aware of what's going on in your world, but not get caught up with which side you are on. Remember that we are dealing with people. While we may have our own opinions about issues, we are all a part of the human race, or the same body of water so to speak. Allowing the differing opinions to overwhelm you is like getting struck by a giant ocean wave. Of course, things will bother you because we are all human. Be like water, be aware, but do not allow yourself to get sucked in. A good place to learn more about not getting sucked in is in author Jordan Peterson's book *12 Rules for Life: An Antidote to Chaos,* where he describes how we can resist being pulled into what others are thinking.

BEND IN THE RIVER

Have you ever been around someone who scrambles when things go wrong but can't seem to get anything done? That was Buddy. He would get frantic and freak out under stress. His mind tried to problem solve but it was like a pond. If you had a stick and stirred the dirt at the bottom, it would make mud and the water would become unclear and murky... that was Buddy.

He often overcompensated for his stress by creating more anxiety for himself. He was hyper-focused on the problem or, in many cases, his apprehension over a problem. He approached people this way, both strangers and friends and family. If it was a stranger, he felt they had dishonorable intentions. In personal relationships, he didn't trust anyone due to past problems and experiences. He could not get beyond himself because he wasn't willing to change from problem thinking to solution thinking. If Buddy had been willing to take the time to breathe, he would be able to gather himself and try solution thinking. He would be able to quiet himself through mindfulness and make tranquil the pond he stirred up. Then, he could see through the water, understanding his problems and issues for what they were versus the problem feeling like the end of the world.

Fortunately, he found a mindfulness center where he took up meditation and yoga. As he developed in skill and experience, he saw what he had been doing to himself. His health actually improved. Because of his past problem thinking, Buddy was having problems such as high blood pressure.

Buddy didn't look at problems as obstacles and issues anymore. He described them as a bend in the river to navigate. He said sometimes the water would be rough, while other times calm, but you have to work with it all. This gave him the ability to remove himself from negative people and change his thoughts. Buddy built stronger relationships that added value to his life. Being the nature of water gave him the clarity and adaptability on how he wanted to live his journey.

CHAPTER 8 - WHAT ARE MU YING AND YOW YING?

In self-defense and situational awareness, it is important to have an idea of what you can do and what your attacker can do. But before you can assess that, you must understand how someone's movement and activity can impact your ability to protect yourself. Knowing this will allow you a better opportunity to stop your attacker.

With this in mind, I want to share Yow Ying and Mu Ying, important concepts from Chinese Kung Fu. While both concepts address awareness, Yow Ying represents the external aspects of Chinese martial arts, while Mu Ying represents the internal aspects. Let's start by looking at Yow Ying.

Earlier in the book, we discussed how a person's positioning can threaten you. When you allow someone to get in your personal space, you limit your ability to protect yourself. This may seem obvious but too often we allow ourselves to be lulled into the belief that we can handle anything. Or we convince ourselves we will be okay because we assume the person won't do anything bad to us or treat us incorrectly. However, we may be making this decision with the only information we have available at that time. You must always be aware of the amount of information you have, no matter what, because it will assist your perception and response time. Movement and leg positioning can also tell you if the person will advance, evade, and if you can counter or improve your own positioning.

Stand in a confident stance.

Let's look at some components of Yow Ying to apply this to your general life.

Ma in the Yow Ying represents footwork in Kung Fu.

Footwork is incredibly important in martial arts to ensure you can move and position yourself in the right stance at the right time.

An example of this in our daily lives can be found in Jordan B. Peterson's book "12 Rules for Life: An Antidote to Chaos." In this book, he speaks of carrying yourself with your shoulders back, upright, and head held high. This practice does two things.

First, it builds your presence by changing how you carry yourself, and second, it changes how people respond to you. Positioning yourself this way in conversation allows others to know your intelligence, to realize that you can be assertive, and enables them to recognize that you can handle yourself. This is a mental and general example of Ma because without a foundation to operate from, people tend to run over you.

Another concept of Yow Ying is Sao. Sao teaches you what you can do when blocking, holding, striking, or evading with the use of your hands. Why is this important? Our hands help us to manipulate the world around us.

This applies to the hands of others, too. If someone is hiding their hands; has their hands clinched; is wrenching their hands; looks distressed; or starts raising them to strike, grab or hold you; you must be aware this is happening. This awareness is important so you know what you can do or can't do to stop them.

The life lesson here is that you are always using your mind to manipulate the world around you. If you choose not to take control, you will just have to take what you receive. Now on the other hand, if you manipulate the world around you, you will create what you receive. There is a saying: "Drive the car; don't let the car drive you."

The next concept Sun deals with generating power from the torso. You turn to strike or grab using the movement of your shoulders and torso, which allows you to watch the other person's positioning. Sun also allows you to utilize how your torso connects with your upper and lower body to generate power in everything. This assists you in holds, throws, and strikes while still allowing you to maintain control of your body. Here, the life lesson is about connection. Just as your torso connects and works with the arms and waist, you must connect with people who are going in the same direction that you are. This builds your energy and means you are moving in a positive and growing direction.

Yow, or the waist, is also a strong connection point to your upper and lower body from which Sun (the torso) operates. By understanding how your waist can be used to keep your balance through movement so you can power through the rotation for punches and kicks, you can be more effective in self-defense.

Just like your waist, there are people in your life that can propel your energy and take you next level. Ask yourself, "Who inspires me? Do I have a mentor?" You have to find a person who takes you in the right direction. Make sure just like a belt, they fit and coordinate with the direction where you need to go.

Ngan, which represents your eyes, allows you to read the movements of your attacker and counter them before they achieve their goals. Ngan helps you to neutralize or evade their attack. From a situational awareness standpoint, your eyes allow you to observe the other person's breathing, eye movements, and general nonverbal activity to assess their possible actions.

In everyday terms, this translates to not being blind to what is going on around you. As Maya Angelou said, "When people show you who they are, believe them." Learn to read the nonverbal communication of the people around you. Ask what is going on with someone directly if you have a relationship with them, and research through others about someone if you don't. This is recommended because it is too easy to be blindsided by failing to pay attention to the people around you.

Now let's look at the Mu Ying or internal aspects of Chinese Martial arts.

Energy (Chi) is breathing, described as a vital force, as without it we would cease to live. For the sake of our discussion, we will look at it in two ways: First, controlling your energy to excel at what you do, and second, disrupting the energy of your opponent. If you are constantly working on your physical fitness by exercising, your body will operate better even under stress. If you knock the wind out of your opponent or they tire out in pursuit of you, you win. You can also impact your energy emotionally, so make sure you train yourself to control or focus your emotions to assist you, not impede you, in self-defense.

If you want to enjoy life, do whatever you can at whatever stage you are in to stay positive and physically fit to embrace the life you have been given. Public speaker Paris Robinson shares with audiences how he was shot four times in his chest. As a result, he was told he would always need someone to take care of him because he was paralyzed from the shoulders down. He heard an inner voice one day that told him, "If you don't fight for your life, you will die." He took that to heart. Over the next two painstaking years, he worked hard and regained his upper body function. Not only is this a great accomplishment, but he has also used his experiences as an example of how you can create and appreciate your life. He has competed in bodybuilding, worked with patients who have become paralyzed, and provided wheelchair sessions for able-bodied people that generate a stronger appreciation for what we have and can do. Paris reminds his audience to enjoy life and always make the most of it.

Professional speaker Paris Robinson, center, with Dan Thurmon, former president of the National Speakers Association on his left, and Brian Muka, speaker and coach, on his right.

Ging is a refined force. To illustrate this, picture yourself propelling an arrow. You can pick up and throw an arrow with your bare hand, but you probably won't hit your target. Your throw will not be a refined force because it will be limited due to the method used. Using your hand, you do not have as powerful a thrust as you would if you used a bow. By using a bow to propel the arrow, however, you are able to create a force multiplier with strong direction. Your arrow reaches the same goal and it does so with increased power. You can use refined force to evade an opponent by being lighter on your feet in motion by using a focused effort.

Just as in martial arts, using Ging or refined force in our daily lives takes focus. Without focus, we can't truly accomplish our dreams, which require goals, measurement, and progressive review to be achieved.

Ask yourself, how strong is the refined force in your life? Are you reaching every result for which you aim? Are you making excuses and missing the mark? Are you leading people in the wrong direction due to your lack of focus? Remember your life is not just about you, but also how you impact others.

The concept of Sen is about awareness. We have discussed awareness from various aspects in martial arts, including Orient in the OODA Loop and Kadima.

Pay attention to all of your senses and your gut. Often, we choose to ignore what we feel. Even when we get a feeling something isn't right, we go ahead and enter a room, house, garage, or alley to prove to ourselves we are not scared or to show we can handle it. These "gut" feelings happen for a reason, however, and we need to listen to them. These feelings have kept us as humans alive throughout time, so pay attention and operate accordingly.

This also goes for your senses. Live in an enlightened way by being aware of your surroundings.

A word of caution, however, about being hyperaware of your surroundings. Are you living a heightened and aware life, not just to protect yourself but to enjoy life? For some, it can be easy to fall into a trap of being too risk-averse and limiting your actions. Keep yourself from boxing in your awareness through your own thoughts or adopting those of others. Be willing to branch out, try new things, and discover (or become aware) of the life around you.

Daom or fearlessness speaks to your ability to be able to have a warrior heart regardless of the facts of the situation. As we stated before, you have to move forward or use your Kadima mindset to survive an attack. Often in a fight, the person who wants to survive and win will succeed. But if you lose heart, and focus on the odds of your not winning due to the size, skill, or other advantages the other people may have, you will lose. With this in mind, walk in fearlessness and live.

If you ask any highly successful person if their journey to the top was easy, not one will say yes. As the saying goes, "People see the glory but they don't know the story." In other words, there are many people who became successful who were initially denied opportunities again and again, but we don't hear about their struggles. These successful people were fearless, sometimes were even brought to tears, but they kept going. Perhaps you have heard about billionaires who started their journey living homeless in their car after losing everything. They had to start over again and they succeeded. Or you may know of a celebrity who was a rising star in a sport. When an injury stops their career, which would seem like a road to failure, it ended up instead moving them to a higher and greater destiny elsewhere. The list of examples goes on and on. Embrace fearlessness in your approach to life and don't let anything stop you.

Sic or knowledge speaks to what you know about yourself and what you know about the other person. In martial arts, it has been said that if you know yourself

100% and you know your opponent 100%, you should win 100% of the time.

As we discussed with the OODA loop, if you know what you can effectively do with your skillset, and then apply that understanding through your knowledge of what the other person can do, you will be successful. Knowledge and understanding are key to any success in life, so always challenge yourself to learn, develop, grow, and share.

This mindset moves everyone forward. When we work together it propels all of us to new heights. Remember, as long as you are alive, you have the opportunity to build a new you. No matter what you have been through, strive for your best.

LIVE BEYOND WHAT IS TO WHAT COULD BE

Paris would tell you he is a normal guy that makes the most of life. He is a motivational speaker that goes into hospitals, detention centers, prisons, and nursing homes to inspire and motivate people. Why is he different? Because he is a paraplegic. He lost his ability to walk from a gunshot. He had to discover the internal and the external aspects of himself in order to not be a victim but be a warrior. He fought physically and mentally for years so that he could go from being bedridden to bodybuilding. Paris went from mentally being ready to die to realizing he had too much to offer others.

How did this come about? Paris had to understand what he could and couldn't do then exceed his own expectations. He went from feeling trapped by drug addiction, the prison system, and being paralyzed to becoming completely drug-free, inspiring others, and showing people how freely they can live. To understand where you are and do something about it takes a mental and physical change. He developed his public speaking skills and his outlook on life because people need to see hope and recognize they are more than what they see now. He speaks with people one on one, in groups, and in larger audiences. He developed his body from being in bed to core strength in a wheelchair playing basketball to bodybuilding and creating a wheelchair challenge.

With the wheelchair challenge, you go a day with Paris through the city in the life of someone in a wheelchair. He teaches you how to navigate, cope, and deal with the challenges of living in a wheelchair. But most importantly, he trains you on how to have a higher outlook on life. Paris is not about just surviving but living well and being able to appreciate life with all its possibilities. Just think, if Paris had not developed the internal and external aspects of himself, could he have inspired and motivated people who are emotionally or physically disabled by the conditions in their lives? Could he have uplifted people to have gratitude and set higher heights for their journey no matter what? Finding it in your heart and having the will to live beyond what is to what could be makes him not a victim but a warrior.

CHAPTER 9 - HOW CAN I
LIVE LIFE UNAFRAID?

Have you ever noticed deer romping in a field? Or watched kittens while they play? These animals are very aware of using all their senses. They are focused on the action at hand, whether it is "horseplay" with fellow creatures or concentrating on attacking their "prey." But at the same time that they are honed in on their activities, these animals are still paying attention to circumstances around them. If the deer in the field are playing but suddenly hear a noise, they will stop their actions, listen, and look around them. They have an awareness. Yet they don't stop enjoying life.

Many of us live our lives in fear. Once we have a strong situational awareness mindset, once we realize there are threats we have been ignoring, we go right into hypersensitivity mode. I call this "living on red alert," the opposite of the "red alert on safety" concept I shared earlier. What I mean by living on red alert is that we live our lives as though we are always at a red light, so we constantly hit the brakes. When we are hypersensitive, we become jumpy and overreact.

But being aware is not the same as being hypersensitive. You can be aware of "red" situations but you can still enjoy life around you. Instead of living on red alert, you can choose to live on green.

For an example of living on green, let's say you live in the woods. When you walk near your home you may enjoy the wind blowing through the leaves and the fresh air. But while you are on your walk, you can still be aware that you could come across something that might be dangerous. On your walk, you logically know you might encounter a bear, a cougar, or a snake. When you embark on your walk, you recognize there are threats, but that's all you need to do. Just be aware while you walk. You don't have to be so threatened that you don't enjoy or notice the other pleasurable things that are out there as well.

You can enjoy a walk while remaining alert for potential issues.

This same scenario can be your mode of operation whenever you are in public, say, at a mall, with friends. You want–and should–enjoy life to the fullest. Wonderful activities like spending time with friends and family are something you should attract in your life.

When you recognize that life can bring sorrow and pain, but it can also bring joy, you realize the pain you experience will give you a greater appreciation of the joy. We deal with the pain that allows us to become stronger and possibly help someone else. Allowing fear through hypersensitivity, and never trying new experiences, means you make your life a perpetual state of pain and avoidance.

How do you live on the green while also being mindful? One way to experience life is to be casually aware. For example, you can use reflective surfaces for awareness, such as using a mirror at the back of a restaurant or the reflection from a window to observe your surroundings. It can be subtle, as you can just check the reflection every now and then, to remain observant.

When you go to your car and you are unlocking it, are you aware of the people and other vehicles around you? Be aware of the bad stuff, of course, but also look for the things that bring you joy. Perhaps on the way to unlock your car you see someone you haven't seen for years. That can make for a joyful reunion. Or you might see a hilarious sticker on someone's window that gives you a much-needed laugh. I've heard it said, "You never know what angels you might be entertaining."

When you are engaging with a person, say while you are at a store, practice being courteous, and ask how the other person is doing. While they are speaking, keep your eye contact with them. Not only does this practice let you know where someone's mind is, but it also lets the person know that you see and acknowledge them. Engage in a friendly way and you could even change their mood. This is often described as "breaking the ice." When someone is giving you service, engage them, and say "Thank you," even at a brief face to face encounter like at a tollbooth.

Breaking the ice is a valuable practice to use in a tense situation. I've seen situations where someone will directly confront someone by "getting up their face" when they are displeased with what they are being told. But without assessing the other person's mood, you never know if that person could snap in reaction. There are two approaches to this: problem thinking and solution thinking. Problem thinking means you only focus on the negatives and what could go wrong. Through solution thinking, which means evaluating the possibilities, you can start formulating new approaches. I challenge you to choose solution thinking.

For example, let's say you are parked in the parking lot. A man pulls up and double-parks behind you as you are ready to leave. You might watch to see where he's going. If it is apparent he's planning to stay parked for a while, you might say, "Hey, what are you doing?" If he becomes belligerent and yells, you can choose to use your solution thinking mindset by de-escalating the situation by saying something that takes him off guard. One example is, "Sorry to bother you, but my wife is expecting any day and I need to be able to leave at moment's notice." That kind of comment gives a reason for the person to change their attitude. Or you could choose to say, "I was just leaving. Do you want the space?" Likely the person who was angry will change their mindset when you make that offer.

You have a choice about how to handle a difficult situation.

Making others feel at ease by just talking with them is a good strategy to develop relationships in addition to diffusing escalating events. I've seen guys behaving like an alpha male, potentially alienating and even upsetting others around them. While the only way they know how to act is through anger, you still have a choice about how you react to them. A better way to think is, "I don't need to challenge your alpha-ness. I just need you to respect mine."

Some of this may sound like basic knowledge, but with age and experience we sometimes block out our instincts and let situations cloud our judgment. Dogs and children often have keener instincts because they do not have the social conditioning we have as adults.

In recent times, the "Me Too" movement has put a spotlight on women who were harassed by men. While the momentum from "Me Too" has created a renewed sense of dedication to making workplaces safe from these kinds of terrible encounters, there has been some backlash from thin-skinned guys. Guys might become hypersensitive because they are scared of being falsely accused or are afraid of unwittingly saying or doing something that could be construed as crossing a line. This sort of hypersensitivity can be described as, "if you're not for me, you're against me" or an "all or nothing" mentality.

In fact, hypersensitivity can occur even if nothing has happened. For example, police officers have to be aware of others and their surroundings in order to be effective in their jobs. I admire the police and know they have a difficult job every day. Police training is beneficial to keep the police force sharp and help them practice difficult scenarios in a controlled environment. Sometimes members of law enforcement may seek training outside of their department run by personnel who teach that something bad is always going to happen. This training can even imply that "Everyone is a threat!" While we want our police force to be aware, we don't want to train them to overreact.

Profiling people according to race is another form of hypersensitivity. One day my brother-in-law, who is African-American, was driving a Honda. He went into a convenience store where several squad cars pulled him over. They said they stopped him because he "fit a description." While he knew he had nothing to hide, he was still scared to tell the police that they couldn't search his vehicle. In this case, his hypersensitivity was for his own safety. If you are racially profiled, having your hands on the steering wheel with license and registration is a smart idea.

Because we act in certain ways, we can control how we react in martial arts. There is a difference between self-defense, martial arts, and fighting. When you are trained, and you use self-defense when someone starts something, you have a strategy to halt it from progressing. Fighting itself is all about winning or losing. Different martial arts have different uses outside of defending one's self, however. For example, martial arts can be used to raise a nation with better health, provide a sense of being, and offer a plan for being more productive. Lain Abernethy created something called a martial map which shows the similarities and differences between the three main types of martial arts which illustrates this.

Some people think, "I know karate, so I should be able to take on anybody." However, thinking this way isn't always the best way to defend yourself. Sometimes the smartest move is to be able to assess the situation and make it home!

How can you negotiate a situation so you do not have to live afraid? First, use your mind as it is your best tool. About 75-80% of assaults could be avoided through situational awareness.

And look at life for what it is. Life is filled with wonder, possibilities, and opportunities. But it also has tragedies. Be aware of life as a whole as there will always be threats along the way. But you are here for a reason, and there is so much to appreciate. You have the power, and you get to decide. Are you going to make the choice to enjoy your life?

YOU CAN BE WATCHFUL
AND STILL ENJOY LIFE

Many people live like the next bad thing is about to happen to them and they don't know how to be safe. At least, that was how Sandra was living. You name it, Sandra was not going to be caught unprepared because she lived on red alert. She had security systems in her home and car. Also, she carried a stun gun for shopping or going places at certain times because it wasn't safe (at least in her eyes). She didn't look at people, events, or places as opportunities for enjoyment, but only for what could go wrong. She stayed stressed out and hardly enjoyed anything.

Sandra felt the safest barricaded in her home with the alarm on, regardless of the time of day. She lived in a very safe neighborhood, but as she would say, "you never know." In public, everything was a threat to her including cars, people, older buildings, weather (because if you can't see through the weather, you can't see the threat), etc... She would overreact towards a stranger in a store or on a sidewalk.

The interesting thing about Sandra is that she was not always like this. Her extreme attitude about safety developed over time. Even though she never had anything traumatic happen to her or anyone she cared about, she did watch a lot of crime dramas and videos on Facebook as well as Youtube, so this may have had an impact. She had a home gym set up including a treadmill so she didn't have to run outside or go to a health club.

When she dated, she always drove and would never let a guy know where she lived. As a matter of fact, only her family and best friend knew where she lived. When it came to work, she wouldn't get in the elevator if there were too many people or if it was just one person whom she didn't know. She would just wait for the next one. If she was short for time, she would take the four flights of stairs needed to get to her floor. Lunch was always at the same place, at the same time, and she ate the same meal because she had to control all the variables. Her coworkers couldn't convince her to go out with them, not even for birthdays.

Sandra was dating a guy for three months and again, they would never ride together in the same car. After seeing a movie (during which she always had to sit in a specific location in the theater), they would usually go to dinner.

During their meal, Sandra would always be polite to her servers because she felt they may sabotage her food. One time, her date asked if she had ever traveled abroad. Her reply was, "I don't do planes, trains, boats, or overseas." He told her she was missing out, but she said she could get the same experience watching it on her HDTV. He pointed out that it wasn't the same and she quickly asked what his point was. Sandra had never even gone outside of the state she lived in. She was raised, went to school, and worked in the same state her entire life. Her boyfriend pointed out that there was nothing wrong with that but the world had so much more to offer through experience. And, there was no experience like living it for yourself. In other words, to see some of these places on television or the big screen pales in comparison to the real-life experience. Plus, he wanted to have these life experiences with her.

She was really hesitant but agreed to start venturing outside of her box by going to his favorite Indian restaurant. Within months, she participated in unplanned events that he came up with spontaneously. Six months later, she took a trip to New York by plane! And within a year, she traveled with him to Cancun, Mexico, for vacation.

Now you may look at this situation and say that the determining factor was the boyfriend. However, she had had boyfriends in the past. Then you may say this guy must be the one. Nope, that relationship only lasted another five months after Cancun but she took a trip to Rome eight months after that. So what was it that changed her outlook? It was Sandra, pure and simple. Sure, her boyfriend sparked thought and interest but she found a reason (a powerful why) that was strong enough to make a change. She reflected on what she had in comparison to the opportunities she truly had in front of her. She found it in herself to do and have something different. She realized she could still be aware of danger because the reality is out there, but she could enjoy the beauty of life at the same time.

She said when she had her epiphany, "I always watch everyone around me and if I'm driving, I want to know who is behind me, especially at a traffic light. I'm concerned if they are following me or have ill intent. One day I was at a light and watching for the same things. I watched a couple in the car behind me through my rearview mirror. They weren't speaking to each other and even looking away from each other. Then the driver turned and looked at his spouse and rubbed her cheek. She turned back at him smiling and then held his hand. I realized by my watching I was keeping myself safe but caught a moment of love and affection. That told me I could have the same. When I reached my destination, I walked across the parking lot. I did my usual look around to see what was around me and guess what I saw? My favorite high school teacher, Mrs. Starks. I hadn't seen her since high school. I was able to say 'hi' and she remembered me and my siblings. We had a great visit and plan on reconnecting as she has retired and only lives 10 minutes away from me. I never would have seen her unless I kept a watchful eye as usual. That day showed me that I could apply my watchful skill set while enjoying life at the same time. So, I said to myself, 'What else is there that I don't want to miss out on?'... And the journey continues."

CHAPTER 10 - WHAT IS THE REAL TRICK OF CLOSE-UP MAGIC?

During a professional seminar, my cohorts and I witnessed a magician who asked a lady to sit in a chair in front of him. By switching his hands, he pulled out tissues of various colors which he made "disappear" in front of her eyes. To the lady, it appeared that the objects were disappearing. During this experience, the magician asked those of us in the audience to remain quiet. We were able to see what was really going on because the magician and the woman were at a distance. As a result, the entire audience could see all of the angles of activity. From a distance, we saw him hide the tissues in a way that made them look as if they had vanished. While the lady experienced shock and awe, the audience was later able to chuckle because we saw the magician's "tricks" and knew exactly what happened.

The real trick of close-up magic is that what you can't see can fool you. Often the things we see aren't what they seem, and we need to have a more watchful eye in order to win.

Magicians know what you can't see can fool you.

It is so important to be aware of what is going on within your circle and around it. You can't just keep your head down and think everything will be okay. Nor can you be so caught up in activity around you that you are blindsided or enthralled to the point of missing danger or warning signs. This is vital to your success. But, if you aren't paying attention because you are distracted, you have made yourself a victim.

I attended a presentation by a keynote speaker named Kevin McCarthy. He wrote a book called *Blind Spots: Why Good People Make Bad Choices,* which chronicled how as an officer in a company, he was working so hard that he had a blind spot to what was actually going on.

The actions of another company officer caused Kevin to serve time in federal prison because of his position in the company. He said if he had paid attention to the activities around him, he could have avoided heartbreak and pain for himself and his family.

I am not saying that you are always going to notice everything. For example, a gentleman shared a story that resonated with me. He said he is always watching out in parking lots, but one day while he was getting into his vehicle, a guy immediately walked up to his window and asked him for help. He was startled because he never saw the guy approach, and yet there he was. The man shared that this meant he realized the other guy had been watching him and noticed that the man didn't see him. Unfortunately for this guy, the storyteller was prepared. He acted as if he were grabbing a firearm from out of his vehicle. When the other guy saw this man's actions in the car, he immediately backed off. The man was still really bothered that he didn't see the guy approach him and it shook him up. I complimented him on his quick thinking and response.

Be aware of your surroundings.

The moral here is you can't catch everything, but you want to prepare as best as you can. As we discussed in the previous chapter, you can't be overly stimulated, enthralled, or ignorant of what is going on around you. It could cost you your security, freedom, or life. Let's review that from a mental attribute side.

Consider your relationships with your family, your coworkers, the public, and your friends. How often have you been engrossed or oblivious to what is occurring in your everyday life? If you fail to pay attention, you find yourself missing cues to what is actually going on around you. It could end in a chuckling event like the woman and the magician, or it could end with you in a federal prison, or worse. You have to make sure you are navigating your life or it will navigate you. Author Jim Lovell said, "There are people who make things happen, there are people who watch things happen, and there are people who wonder what happened. To be successful, you need to be a person who makes things happen." There is no doubt that you are on the earth to accomplish something so it is worth your while to pay attention.

Keep your eyes open to know what is going on around you. Give yourself the space you need, and the time to reflect and build strategies. Do check-ins against what you think you know and consider the possibilities. This is not to say that challenges will not still be present. If you look at the history of people to create, explore, and innovate, we can accomplish anything by evaluating the world around us and making the necessary shifts to be successful.

THE BIGGER PICTURE

Alexis said, "If you stay ready, you'll always be ready." She always pointed out that if you are ahead of the game in the knowledge of a situation or how to deal with one, then you won't be absent of a solution or strategy. She was an old soul, a listener and a watcher. Alexis always paid attention when older people spoke because they had the experience that she didn't have. She watched what got her friends and siblings into trouble and she was constantly learning from their mistakes. As a member of a track team, she welcomed the opportunity to go last so she could improve her form by the corrections she saw the coach give others. Then when it was her turn, she looked like a superstar who knew how to do it all along.

When Alexis went to college, she kept observing people. She recognized the signs of guys who want to befriend her for the wrong reasons or girls who wanted her to join in their cliques. She also watched out for her girlfriends. Often, they were so caught up by the "close-up magic" that they were blinded to the fact that a guy was trying to take advantage of them or that their judgment was impaired because they had too much to drink. She made sure if they came together, they left together. If her friends became confrontational about leaving together, they always came back apologizing because trouble occurred. Alexis was there for them even after trouble. So I guess you could say, if she considers you a friend, you were a friend. Now you may think "this sounds too good to be true." Is Alexis some kind of saint, a Mary Poppins "do-gooder," or just a boring person in other people's business? Actually, she was quite active in college organizations including leadership positions. She loved to dance and enjoy a fun party. Alexis dated, had a romantic interest, and appreciated the opportunities that college life provided. So, it was just as easy for her to fall into life's potholes as it was for anyone else. But no matter how she felt emotionally, she acted on wisdom and not by her feelings. Paying attention to the signs, the red flags, the cues of others, and raising her awareness well before the problem presented itself made it so that there was no close-up magic she couldn't figure out or ask for advice about before she had to engage with the situation. This was and continues to be her strategy for life.

CHAPTER 11 - HOW CAN
I BUILD ARMOR?

Americans love fashion! Often our clothing choices are for looks and not for utility. But when it comes to self-defense you need to be aware of what you have on, and whether your clothing can be used for or against you.

Throughout history, during warfare, we have used various coverings to protect ourselves from blades, bullets, and bludgeon attacks. Whether it was chain, metal, or bamboo armor, we used wearable protection along with shields and various other weapons to defend ourselves. While these may not make news in the fashion world, we must still be aware that what we wear can either help or hinder our ability to survive an attack.

Why is it important to build armor mentally and physically in self-defense?

The physical part of your clothing "armor" can be vital in an attack. You may not have considered this, but you can wrap a scarf, a sweater, a light jacket, or sarong around your arm in case you have to break a window or defend yourself against a knife. With training, you can also use this clothing to choke your attacker or immobilize them. If you are dressed in layered clothing, it will be harder for an attacker to cut through to your abdomen or chest with a slashing cut. If the person attacks with a straight stab and you are not already moving away from it, no matter what you are wearing it can cause a lot of damage. So again, this is situational, but the fewer clothes you wear the more vulnerable you are.

Be aware that a scarf, tie, sarong, sweater, coat, or jacket can also be used to grab you, pull you off from your balance or choke you, depending on your attacker's abilities. A coat can even be used against you by pulling it over your head and attacking you while you are bound. Knowing this, you must be prepared to prevent this from happening. Train to make quick counters for striking while they have a hold, or make them release their hold. Be aware of what can happen and train to be ready for it. If you are interested in learning more, there are self-defense programs that teach you how to use your clothing. There are also companies that sell attire that is resistant to knives, fire, and other hazards.

Consider that your clothing can be used as a weapon or to defend yourself.

You may be surprised to learn that physically many people are walking around with "bikinis" on! Yes, I mean both men and women, and not just at the beach. Why do I say this? These people are exposed to the elements around them because they did not prepare to wear clothing that protects them. Whatever comes at you, including rain, dust, gases, storms, and lightning, will touch and impact you when you are outdoors because of what you are wearing. What would happen if you were pelted with large hail? What happens when UV rays damage your skin? How will you react if sand blows into your eyes? If you fall while wearing a bikini and create an abrasion, puncture, or laceration, this occurs because of your clothing choice. These are all consequences of improper apparel.

Mentally, people and the stimuli that generally bombard us daily can have an impact the same way that harmful substances can injure us physically. Whether we are engaged in a conversation or viewing social media, television, or YouTube, we are always receiving messages that make us feel better or worse about ourselves. The importance of using mental armor comes in because it impacts how you navigate or respond to all these messages. Often people who have lower self-esteem want to draw attention to themselves to show off. These people may shelter themselves so they don't have contact with others. While hiding behind their screen images, they want you to feel bad about comparing yourself to their "perfect lives" so they can feel superior.

When we have on mental armor, we are shielded from negativity but we cannot remove all of the elements. Mental armor just allows us to operate in our daily lives in the face of this negativity. If I have on a protective vest that is puncture and bullet resistant, I can operate with further confidence because I know the level of impact the person can have on me. Without it, I'm more vulnerable. So just like physical armor, mental armor gives you more opportunity to assess your situation and adapt to how you need to respond.

You can build up armor mentally so you can practice keeping your wits about you in the event of an attack. Using the OODA loop, as we discussed previously, is a form of mental armor. During the engagement, you choose whether you de-escalate the conflict verbally or escalate it physically. When you make this decision, your thoughts and emotions must be in concert with what you are doing. You will not be convincing if your response is verbal and then you second guess your physical ability. You'll be more concerned about being struck than surviving.

As we have discussed, I want you to develop a warrior mentality and make sure you make it home. Consider this question to help you get there. What would your world look like if you didn't make it home and who would be impacted? How would it affect the people who depend on you? How would their security be impacted if you aren't able to make it home? What about people that you mentor or are friends with? Are you acting in a way that they will want to turn to in critical times? What about your dreams and desires? Are you willing to lose them because of an attack?

Your goal is always to make it home alive.

We have so many experiences and people to live for. We can't afford to voluntarily allow ourselves to become the victim of an attack. This is not an option. You can learn and develop your ability to create a warrior mindset. This applies to the verbal aspects of self-defense, too.

For example, let's say a lady is walking down the street. As she turns a corner, she notices a man who instinctively makes her decide to give herself more walking space between them. The guy notices, becomes upset and starts yelling at her, asking, "What's your problem?" If her response to the man was, "I was recently assaulted," the guy may apologize to her for his strong response. If instead, she responded by saying something that would incite the person further, such as, "You look suspicious to me," it could add more tension to an already uncomfortable situation. As you can see, a proper verbal response can make a difference, so be prepared mentally.

Consider your response to everyday situations.

We can also place "armor" to shield against our own negative thoughts. Be aware that you can always choose knowledge over emotion to prevent yourself from feeling down. If a guy sees another guy who is buff and becomes intimidated by the guy's looks, he is not thinking about his own value and attributes. Nor is he congratulating the guy for all the work he did to become that way. The same goes for a gorgeous lady. A woman may see another beautiful woman and think to herself, "Wow, she must have everything. I wish I could be her." This woman, through comparing herself with the other woman, isn't thinking about all the gifts she has. She has allowed her feelings to blind her from her own gifts, and it impacts her emotionally. With proper mental armor, this woman can find things she likes about the gorgeous woman and can celebrate with her. And she can feel gratitude for the gifts she has received.

Think about your own gifts instead of comparing yourself to others.

We are pulling in numerous ideas and stimulation that impact how we run our daily lives. Some are positive while others are not. When we watch programming, view social media, and interact in conversations that are actually counterproductive to what we say we are and where we want to go in life, it can harm us. For example, you might say you want to get out of debt, but then if you don't budget and change your money management strategies, you will continue to need help. If you want to change your career and possibly start a business, but you don't spend your free time developing and learning what you need to become successful, you won't get anywhere. If you say you want to lose weight but keep the same habits, you will stay at the same weight. I can go on and on with examples, but the point is, our world doesn't change until we do. Mental armor gives us an opportunity to objectively look at what we want to accomplish and develop a game plan. Even while the world is sending millions of stimuli at us daily, we can still stay on the correct path because we have a foundation, a mental armor from which we can operate.

EARNING YOUR BELT

In my previous book *Grounded: Life Lessons*, in Chapter 5, "Being Rooted," we discussed the roots above and the roots below as a metaphor for life. As we all know, the seed and root system below are the determinant as to what can come above. We can see it as the fruit of the labor below. Depending on the soil and elements such as sun, rain, wind erosion, and animals, it can be a challenge for the seed to become full-grown and fruitful. The farmer plants seeds in more than just one in an area because the chance of each one coming to fruition is limited. Now think about this: it is what you don't see that makes it successful. What you can see is the fruit of what it went through to get there. In *Grounded: Life Lessons*, this process is described as the internal you, while the fruit is the external you. Both are important. You develop your armor internally by what goes on underground, through what you had to do to get rooted and beat the challenges in your life. The fruit is an external result, therefore the expression of what you accomplished from your development. So if you have never internally developed from adversity, you will not have the armor internally to deal with what you may face. The fruit of what you have become is displayed externally by the way you carry yourself, the way you deal with others, and the way you express yourself which all speak to the armor you have developed. When you can express yourself without becoming emotional, people will have to contend with the fact they couldn't get past your armor. It can also be said that the armor you wear when you present yourself warns others you are a force to be reckoned with and not to be taken for granted.

When it comes to plants, which do you think would be stronger, the one that had to deal with the elements or the one grown in a hydroponics case? Both become full-grown so there shouldn't be a difference, right? You might think they should even taste the same, too. Well, let's look at some of the differences. Sun exposure, soil nutrient type, and water quality are some of the most impactful variables. I mention this because all of these factors play a part in the development of the plant. Therefore, internal challenges, conditions, and diversity impact the plant in the same way that challenges impact your internal armor.

In martial arts, reaching a black belt level is similar to graduating high school. This says that you now have the skills to train at a higher level. And depending on your school and your teacher, you may have a standard diploma or an advanced diploma from a high school standpoint. But what does it take to reach black belt? Blood, sweat, and tears from trial and error to develop skills that take dedication, commitment, and an enduring spirit. But once you achieve it and wear it, it represents the armor you developed to reach that level.

There is a reason there is a belt system as each represents a level that has been attained. The reason the white belt is at the beginning is the fact that you are fresh and new. You are starting the journey but haven't accomplished or been through anything yet. Before multi-level belt systems were used in some forms of martial arts, there were only two types: a white belt and dirty belt. The dirty belt represented your years of training. The longer those years went on, the more tattered the belt became. So again, a white belt represented the beginning while a black belt represented what you went through to develop the armor needed to achieve the ability to learn at a higher level.

It's funny that anything in life that is worthwhile is a process, not a "give me." So whatever stage you are at in life, wear your armor and keep developing it by continuing to challenge yourself. It will only protect you and make you stronger for the next level of challenges.

CHAPTER 12 - HOW DO I TAKE THE OPPONENT'S "REAL ESTATE"?

Sometimes to protect themselves, people will walk around with hard looks on their faces or present themselves in an unfriendly manner. Their purpose for this behavior is to tell you, "Hey, don't mess with me, because as you can see, you don't want any of this!" They act this way so they can control the space or "real estate" around them. This is sometimes a game of "opossum." While some people act this way in the hopes that you never mess with them, but are really insecure, there are others behaving in this manner who are genuinely looking for trouble. You don't always know who is who.

We are going to look at how you can take your opponent's real estate, and how to prevent someone from taking yours. First, please realize that not everyone is coming from the same mindset. Some people may have had bad experiences in their lives that caused them to put up this warning wall. Others may have been taught that acting tough is the way you survive in the street. Let's look at some examples.

When a guy and girl walk past one another, and the girl smiles, the guy might think the girl is interested in him, when actually she may just be trying to be nice. So ladies, use your discretion. When two guys walk past one another, they may size each other up. The first thing one of them can do is to "punch" the other guy with a...smile. "Hello, how are you doing today?" "Good morning!" This lets the other guy know where they're at, that they are confident but not looking for trouble. The other guy will either return the smile, which happens most of the time, or they will not respond.

Sometimes you may run into someone who is from another region or culture. Be aware that what's acceptable in one area may be perceived differently in another. Someone from the South Side of Chicago is likely used to putting on a brave face. If this person visits southern Virginia and is greeted by a smile, they may wonder, "Huh, what's his angle?" without realizing their greetings are regionally different. I encourage you to be prepared no matter how someone reacts, as you are learning information to gain their real estate. If their "tough guy" expression was just a veneer or facade, the person will likely open up to a conversation or just return the smile or greeting. But, if they ignore you or respond in an unkind fashion, **now you know where their head is!** Keep on walking. This assessment is so important because it helps you evaluate your situational awareness and start to learn the other person's intent.

Someone who looks tough may actually be protecting themselves.

Here are three examples of taking someone's real estate with positive results:

- An instructor is approaching a martial arts school. There is construction being done in front of the building so it is not well lit. He sees a guy approaching from his left who appears to be lurking. The instructor initially is unsure of the man's intention. He says 'good evening' and finds out the guy is interested in training, has never been to this school, and arrived early. When the man says to the instructor that he is there early, the instructor knows he is there for training and not for harm.
- An older lady in a coffee shop sees a large man come inside in a rush and she becomes concerned. She feels uncomfortable because

of how the man hurried the coffee shop and because of his size. When he sees her looking at him, the man sets up his computer and looks at her with a smile, explaining it was a rough day. She changes her demeanor and asks if he would like to sit at her table to power his computer.

- A guy leaves the gym and says, "Hey, how are you doing?" to another man who is walking in. The man brushes him off and goes into the gym. With that, since he wasn't friendly, the guy knows the man's frame of mind and figures out how to deal with him. If at another time they have a conversation, the guy will know how to respond to the man, and perhaps choose not to interact.

- A tourist visiting an international market is being led by a guide. While walking, the tourist accidentally knocks over a wood carving at one of the booths. Immediately, the booth owner rushes to him angrily, yelling, waving his arms in the air, and making violent facial expressions. The tourist steps toward him with his shoulders back, looks the owner directly in the eye, and says, "I apologize, I didn't see it," then says nothing else. All of a sudden, the booth owner changes his demeanor to a smile and asks if he can show the tourist something. Why did the owner start yelling the way he did? He was trying to take the tourist's real estate. His past behavior had shown him that this was an effective tactic to make tourists feel bad and

buy something, but as soon as it didn't work,
he changed his tactic.

Some folks feel they are better than others, whether they have looks, strength, roughness, or fighting ability, you name it. They may carry themselves with arrogance and a bully mentality, and they want to control every situation they are in. They may use manipulation or direct threats, either verbally or physically. As you see, many of these behaviors are learned and they don't necessarily mean people are evil. They just may be trying to manipulate the situation and take your real estate.

What about the person that wants to do you harm? Let's say you are walking and approach a couple. The lady smiles at you and you return the smile. Her boyfriend doesn't like it, however, and approaches you about it. You may go back to "punching" him with a smile, telling him she reminded you of a friend or family member, and then offer to buy them a cup of coffee. Through your friendly exchange, you are de-escalating the situation. You are doing this because you want to help him calm down and because you do not want anyone to get hurt. Some of you may read this and say to yourself, "If that were me, I wouldn't back down. I may step up to confront him." Answer this question: What do you have to lose in the long run for making a bad decision in the short run? Let that be your guide. If everyone goes home unharmed, you have won!

Let's look at a situation where a person won't back down from taking your real estate. They intend to use force as a powerful dimension to hurt, harm, or steal from you. When this kind of situation occurs, you need to recognize red zones and green zones of protection. A red zone is a distance where the person can strike or grab you to achieve their goal. In the green zone, you are out of their grasp. In self-defense, a green zone is a place that limits the person's ability to achieve their goal.

You want to always be in a green zone if at all possible. The first position requires situational awareness (remember the OODA loop!). This can save you before anything happens. Used effectively, you can avoid a confrontation. It may mean you see something and change your route, stay in a store until it is safe to leave, or use awareness of your surroundings so you are able to escape.

When confrontation is inevitable, and you can't stay in your green zone away from the person, you may have to create a green zone. Think about this: When a small child is misbehaving, you may hug them into you tightly so they can't hit or kick you. Or, if you see a gate is open and a barking dog is running towards you, you can hurry to close the gate so the dog can't get through. These are both ways to create a green zone.

In self-defense, you may close the distance to counter-attack and take away the opponent's ability to strike. This is part of the training in Krav Maga. If you are on the ground and the person is on top of you, you can arrest their movement to avoid major strikes from them. In Krav Maga, Ju-Jitsu, wrestling, and other disciplines that train for being on the ground, you can limit the person's actions by pulling them in and controlling their movements. While all of these things take training, they allow you to create a green zone. In all of the disciplines mentioned, you may slip in a punch or strike to get the other person into a green zone position.

Is your opponent in your red zone or green zone?

Maintaining your real estate is important both physically and mentally. Physically, you can check your environment by using situational awareness and communicating to see what the mindset of the individual is. Then you can make decisions accordingly. We don't know the history and thought patterns of strangers, and we aren't always privy to what another person is thinking, so it is good to run this check. Be aware of when someone is trying to take your real estate through mental battles such as how you perceive their body posture, facial expressions, and tone of voice. Their behavior can range anywhere from them having a bad day to them planning an action with ill intent. If the confrontation is going to happen, control your real estate (personal space) by staying out of a red zone. If they are approaching to attack, make your green zone away from them. If it is too late, make your green zone on them with a trained attack such as a crash or burst that increases your ability to survive.

We have discussed the applications of maintaining your real estate in a self-defense situation. Now let's apply this in our daily lives. When we talk about real estate in life, we are talking about your personal space and mental space. For example, there is a profile test that says you are either an extrovert or an introvert. Say you are at work, you are an introvert, and you're a great listener. If people come to your office to talk, they are in your "real estate." There may be times when you are okay with people coming to talk with you, but there are other times when you might need to say, "I'm sorry but I can't talk right now." Here's how you can control these situations.

Number one, not everyone deserves access to your real estate. This includes people who are toxic to your spirit and your life. They will bring down your "property values" and detract from your life. Number two, ensure that people respect your real estate. If people think they can do what they want, when they want, around you, they will. You have to demand respect, even if you have to put a "fence" around yourself. If you don't want your real estate taken over, you have to speak up for yourself or the person will think they have "squatter's rights." Too often people get used to behavior from us that they think means we are okay with them crossing our boundaries. Unless you stand up for yourself, they think, "They love me and I always do this, so it is okay." When you let people cross your boundaries, it will take you double the work to get them out. You live with what you tolerate.

Number three, sometimes you need time alone in your real estate just to enjoy it. Too often we don't allow ourselves to enjoy where we "live." We need quiet time. You may be too busy looking at what someone else has or what you don't. Take the time to enjoy who you are and the space in which you live. Focusing on others and feeling envious doesn't make your life better. Don't be like the person that buys a beautiful home but never spends time enjoying it.

How do you prevent someone from taking your "real estate"?

Last but not least, if you give your real estate away, you are the only one that loses. It may be a long fight before you get it back. Have you ever had a neighbor who wasn't paying attention and crossed over into your yard? You and the neighbor may need to look at the property lines. If it has been a number of years, and you quarrel with your neighbor, it may become an expensive battle involving attorneys to get land back. Look at this land as representing years of your life that you have given away. This "land grab" may result in bad relationships and damage to your self-esteem. You are better off avoiding these relationships rather than making excuses for them. If you know anyone that has ever survived domestic violence or a verbally/mentally abusive relationship, they will always tell you of the length of the journey it took them to rediscover themselves.

Your space, your life, your real estate. Protect it!

DEFEND YOUR
PERSONAL ZONE

Ever had that sibling who was always touching you and you found yourself saying, "Mom, Billy won't stop touching me!" And they would do it again and again. Well, this was Sean's life, even into adulthood. He was always allowing people into his personal zone. If he was riding a bus or a subway, someone would always squeeze in beside him because he wouldn't stand up for himself and let people know he was uncomfortable.

People would step in front of him and then ask Sean, "You don't mind do you?" If he was walking down the street and he saw something or someone he felt threatened by, he would look down or away hoping he didn't have to engage with them. Sean wanted nothing to do with confrontation even when he was growing up. One time when he was cutting his mother's grass, he didn't hear a gang of guys approaching. He stopped as he saw one of them who then confronted him by saying, "We should cut this guy; he thinks he's smart because he's going to college." By the time he knew it, there were at least five guys surrounding him and starting to fight. He looked for someone he could brush by to break their line and run to safety. Fortunately, a kid saw what was happening and ran to Sean's mother. She got in her vehicle which was around the back of the house and drove to the front where the fight was. She ran into the yard where they were and this caused them to separate. She told Sean to get in the car and they sped off. He was on lockdown until he left for college.

This same type of problem occurred in his friendships and relationships. He would let people in, try to be friendly, and often dismiss red flags of behavior that should have told him they weren't good for him. But then, he had to work twice as hard to get them (squatters) out of his life because he had allowed them to be comfortable in his life. He had let them run wild in his life, then always paid for it by being used and emotionally disrupted. The reality of it is that he was the cause of his own pain because he allowed these people to take his real estate.

Sean had seen struggles because his father and mother divorced when he was young. His father slowly stopped coming around because he thought it was more painful for Sean and his siblings. In fact, it was more painful not having his father in his life and Sean looked for relationships to close the void of what he felt he missed out on. He spent time dating a lot of girls over the years and showered them with attention, gifts, and love only to be left heartbroken and told it wasn't going to work out. He eventually got married and felt a special bond with his wife's children because he wanted them to have the father he didn't. As time went on, his wife became abusive. But Sean didn't see confrontation and fighting as a negative, so he only took more of it. He made sure the kids always saw him in a positive light and was there for them. One day, everything came to a head and he couldn't take it anymore. All the years of verbal abuse had taken its toll and he snapped, killing his wife. Even during the trial, the kids and his wife's family spoke on his behalf because of what he endured. He went to prison for manslaughter but was eventually paroled. His life was never the same. As a result of never dealing with the red flags of life and avoiding confrontation as well as seeking help for it, he lost everything.

Cliff, like Sean, is someone who would let things and people get too close to him. He would sometimes complain publicly (not strongly) and sometimes he would complain in private. It would eat at him when he felt something was wrong. The problem for Cliff was that he never looked at the proper remedies to resolve the issues. Either he would say nothing or it was a shouting match in which nothing was resolved. Some remedies Cliff could have taken were addressing issues when he was calmer and putting a plan of action in place if he couldn't get it resolved with a discussion.

One time, Cliff wished he had dealt with things differently, and he later expressed he should have handled it better. He was at home with his family and his neighbors were having a party. It was two o'clock in the morning and the music was blasting. His family told him not to go out there and just call the police, but he told them he would handle it. Leaning over his neighbor's fence, he asked if they knew what time it was, and if they realized that people were trying to sleep. But, because he had never stood up to them before that night, they told him to "take his old ass back to bed." This only inflamed his frustration and he told them to "make him." Two of the ladies came to the fence, one of them cursing him out profusely and putting her hand in his face. Not soon after that, he grabbed her in anger. She broke free running into her house and telling him, "I got something for you!" He went into his house after declaring he wasn't afraid of her or anyone in their house. Fifteen minutes later, the police came and arrested him for assault and battery. He was so devastated that his family had to get him out of jail, and that had to go to court because he didn't work out alternatives. In retrospect, he wished he had called the police as his family requested him.

While Wayne was much different than Cliff, he too was guilty of letting the opponent take his real estate. Wayne was a pillar in the community, always helping, always serving, always giving back to others because he felt blessed that so many had given to him. While Wayne was a sports competitor and was sometimes sponsored, he was never a professional. But with the amount of time he traveled competing and helping judge tournaments, you would have thought he was a professional. He trained others, and developed and supported teams. His wife, on the other hand, didn't feel the same about his activities and had communicated it over the years. He felt he had it all "on lock" and she would always be there. He continued to do his thing as the people he was associating with felt the same as he did. Instead of looking at how his travel was impacting his marriage, he just stayed in concert with people who had the same mindset. They all felt their spouses should understand and be more supportive. Some of them had endured this lifestyle for decades, to the extent that one competitor lost his daughter and his wife divorced him.

One night, Wayne had returned from a trip early and looked forward to surprising his wife only to find her in bed with another man. The man became belligerent and told Wayne to get out of his own house while he was still in bed with Wayne's wife. Wayne lost it. The worst part? Wayne was a trained fighter. He almost beat the man to death. As the man lay on the floor unconscious, Wayne left without even looking back at his wife. He then called the police and turned himself in. After all he had accomplished, all the kids he mentored, the people he helped in the community, he could have lost it all. He no longer had the same opportunities to help others. Several people spoke as character witnesses, including school principals, teachers, and community leaders, and all begged for leniency.

Were these signs in his marriage that Wayne missed? Absolutely! He could have avoided the opponent taking his real estate by taking care of his marriage. Now, no one is saying his wife doesn't hold responsibility for the events that occurred, but he didn't take care to act on the signs his wife expressed. If he had spent time tending to his marriage and lived in balance, maybe they would have been happy together. We will never know. We do know that the path he took made him lose his real estate. Now the question is, who was the real opponent? His failure to face his issues and problems, or the man he found in his bed?

SUMMARY - HOW DOES THIS ALL TIE TOGETHER?

Recently there was a national news report about a man who was a rising star when in school. Having won scholarships to Ivy League schools for undergraduate and law school, it seemed the sky was the limit for him. Unfortunately, this man got into a relationship that ended, leaving him lacking in confidence, and he became homeless. He didn't become homeless because his knowledge, skills, and abilities changed. His situation changed because his thoughts and feelings about himself changed, and that impacted his future. Fortunately, he was later able to get support and rebuild his life.

Finding your true potential means directing your activity and being mindful of the activity around you.

Let's use lawn care as a metaphor for your life. If you maintain and nurture the lawn by feeding it appropriately, addressing weeds, cutting, and seeding, you will have an excellent result with lush, green grass. But if you don't even cut the lawn because you are too busy or don't want to deal with it, what is the result? Have you ever tried to cut grass that is two feet tall with a lawnmower? The mower will constantly choke out and it will take a long, painful time to correct. Plus, depending on where you live, you may have just invited animals to commune in the high grass. Once the grass is cut, the animals are going to go somewhere, and that somewhere may be your home.

Better to address issues in life when they first start with navigation versus with correction after there is a problem. None of this is possible without keeping a watchful eye. You cannot afford to get caught up or ignore what is going on in your life. Many a ship has crashed or run upon rocks because the captain thought without investigating that they had enough room to get by. Your potential in life is too important to be crushed and crashed by something you could have controlled.

Now, I would like to tie together everything we have discussed with a quick recap.

How do I become a protector instead of the one that always needs protecting?

We need to think and act differently to become a protector. Instead of relying on others to protect you, I challenge you to learn to stand up for yourself. Ensure you are developing self-assurance through training and practice, and not through false confidence. Develop your conviction through physical training such as self-defense, and mental toughness through standing up for yourself. Keeping sharp through your training and development is crucial, so continue increasing your knowledge and development in many aspects of your life. Continue to grow and help others to do the same. Protectors can protect because they learned how through knowledge and experience.

How can I create a maximum impact?

Creating a maximum impact is another way to step up and become a protector. Too often we underestimate our ability to bring a maximum impact to a situation because we don't understand what we actually have the power to do. Often it takes training and experience to realize this. But once you understand, this knowledge is yours to act upon. This is true in self-defense and in life. Remember the maximum impact that you create can ripple into the lives of others and change the world.

How can I create a minimal risk for myself?

Self-defense situations are not without risk, but there are ways to minimize the threat level by the means and methods you choose. Proper risk management of the mind involves employing techniques and strategies. You have to limit, avoid, and sometimes transfer the risk that impedes your ability to achieve your vision in life. This often means trading off relationships that don't fit with where you are planning to go.

What is the OODA loop and how can I use it?

By employing the OODA loop, Observe – Orient – Decide – Act, you will gain an upper hand by creating your strategic response to threats and situations. If you choose not to avail this method in your personal life, woe be unto you. You are inviting damage, destruction, and stress that could be avoided. Remember the OODA loop, and use it to your advantage. Another expression similar to using the OODA Loop is, "measure twice, cut once."

What is Kadima and how can I use it to be successful in attacks?

Kadima, the Hebrew word for forward, means meeting situations aggressively and committing allows you to leave safely. This approach allows you to swarm your opponent with techniques and continue to fight until the situation is neutralized. I encourage you to keep the same mindset when dealing with people professionally and personally. Why? It will allow you to think and operate in an assertive manner that eventually brings success, but doesn't stop until the job is done.

What does the Gray Man have to do with my ability to defend myself?

Being the Gray Man means learning how to not be noticed to survive. In self-defense, blending into the crowd allows you to assess your environment. Through clothing and behavior, you can go unseen and therefore avoid many situations. I challenge you to become the Gray Man in every part of your life. Save yourself time and avoid fruitless conversations and scenarios.

What does "being like water" mean for me?

Being the nature of water speaks to the element's flexible nature. Be strong where needed but also be able to yield, too. In self-defense, being like water will allow you to be where you need to be to defend yourself. You will learn where to put your positioning and power. In your daily life, being like water allows you to work in situations and relationships with your goal in mind, while at the same time, being malleable to the needs and communication necessary to work with others. Embrace mindfulness and still the mud.

What are Mu Ying and Yow Yin?

Similar to the internal and external aspects of Chinese Kung Fu, each of us has internal and external attributes that can assist us in negotiating in our lives. It is the application of these attributes that makes us successful. Life has internal and external forces around us impacting the way we live. We must navigate and grow like a plant in the ground, even while rain, wind, and other forces are placed on us. By adapting, we develop stronger roots and thrive to grow stronger and bear fruit.

How can I live life unafraid?

There is so much to receive, see, experience, and give in this lifetime. You only see the opportunities that you are aware of! You can achieve this by living your life unafraid. Like horses, rabbits, dogs, cats, or other animals that commune together to play, enjoy yourself but be aware of your surroundings. When you are in trouble, look to your environment to respond immediately with the tools you have to get away or deal with the conflict. Look at life holistically (yes, the whole thing).

What is the real trick of close-up magic?

Often the things we see aren't what they seem, and we need to have a more watchful eye in order to win. Always try to get the broadest picture of what is going on from the activity and cues in your surroundings. Putting your head down physically or mentally is never advantageous. The problem you see coming is the one you can avoid. Be prepared to act before it is too late by keeping an open eye to avoid a blind spot.

How can I build armor?

Physical and mental readiness will always aid you in a self-defense situation. The higher your fitness level, the better you can respond in movement. Similarly, the higher your mental acuity, the more stable your decision-making abilities will be under threat. Both have to be developed to be effective. But without mental armor you can't create the warrior mentality necessary to fight your way through the attack. This is the same in life. I am not saying to keep a harsh or hard mentality when dealing with people. Instead, have the mental dexterity to shift and protect your mind from people that would have you think less of yourself or become mentally defeated. You must build your armor to endure challenges as you improve your life.

How do I take the opponent's "real estate"?

In defending yourself, be aware of your space or your real estate. If you had a farm that was being invaded (imagine settlers in the Wild West), would you wait until the invaders were on your porch? Or would you start protecting yourself and your family at your property line if you had the means to fend them off? If you answered the property line, you are correct. The deeper invaders come onto your property, the more damage can be done. Instead of dealing with opponents in your space, you want to respond to the conflict by taking their ground before they can cause you damage. This is the same with toxic relationships. As soon as you receive signals that someone is sharing bad ideas or negative energy, you must create a perimeter and defend yourself, or risk being damaged mentally and emotionally.

Through reading this book, my hope is that you have gained a new appreciation for approaching your life. While at any given time, we are exposed to a multitude of threats, we have tools and concepts we can use to address them. By recognizing risks before they become threats, you can live your life in a purposeful manner. I challenge you to live the very best life you can, to live with your "red alert on safety," and enjoy every moment to its fullest.

PUTTING IN THE WORK PROVIDES RICHER RESULTS

People often ask me, "Can you teach me how to defend myself in a couple of classes?" Everyone is always looking for a quick fix, a pill, a couple of exercises that will help them lose weight, or a way to have six-pack abs. Many also want someone else to do the work for them, for everything from meal prep to fully prepared meals delivered to your door. Everyone wants the benefits without the work. And if you try to explain what it will take, it goes beyond their patience or their desire to develop that skill set. Did you know over half of Americans feel they are a disaster in the kitchen and less than that feel competent in preparing a meal?[1]

Why do companies selling diet plans, pills, and videos make so much money without everyone purchasing and receiving 100% results? We like the idea, not the work. Everyone loves a home-cooked meal, yet some never take the time to develop that skill set to prepare a meal, and even more, will say they don't have time for it.

Our lives have become so engulfed in technology and convenience that we are living with a false sense of security. We say, "I live in a safe neighborhood with security systems on my phone, home, and car." We may even use security systems surrounding our children. When it comes to being prepared all you have to do is look at our present national infrastructure in the United States. You can see how entire electrical grids could go down, not because of the lack of intelligent people operating them, but plain old failure. We don't take the time to pass on learning and wisdom.

If you had to survive in the woods, could you? Can you hunt, fish, and navigate the forest? Do you know what to watch out for? Many people can't survive without modern conveniences, including electronics.

I have heard many people complain that kids don't get outside and play "like we used to when we were coming up." They play on gaming systems and watch shows. One of the most disturbing situations that I have seen was during an appointment with a customer. A child kept interrupting even though the mother told him to go put his movie in. It was a horror murder movie. Now, I know that is extreme, but if they are vegging out on an animated kids movie, the

---

1   https://www.theladders.com/career-advice/turns-out-americans-really-dont-know-how-to-cook-anything-but-eggs

result is not much different because they are still in front of a screen.

What is the message here?

In all of these situations, we are failing to develop a skill training mindset. But we say, "it's OK because it isn't hurting anything. I challenge that on every level. We continue to lessen ourselves by what we won't do versus building ourselves by what we will do. We build in one area while saying the other area isn't important. It could be building a career versus building relationships within your family. It could be putting your child in martial arts to learn discipline instead of leaving it up to the school to build on the anchor of what you are doing at home.

Now, don't get me wrong, I love the marvels of technology as much as anyone, but there is something to be said about developing a skill set.

How many of you go hiking, hunting, fishing, boating, rafting, and other outdoor experiences with your family as your parents did with you? All of these activities develop life skills that not only navigate the outdoors but can help you navigate life as well. You may have learned these activities during summer camp, scouting, or with family and friends. When you have a deeper understanding of how to cope with nature, enjoy the fresh air, and how to get to know the people you are with, it enriches you. Did you know studies show that people who spend time outside lead more fulfilling lives, are healthier, and often become great leaders because they can think outside of the box? This only comes with experience that develops an individual to survive and thrive.

Do you remember a relative who could create quilts? It is a skill that dying out in many families because it is no longer passed down from generation to generation. It was a skill that was a labor of love. For those teaching the quilting, it was an opportunity to impart wisdom to those who were learning.

Now, I'm not trying to create a movie scene that you have seen time and time again. You speak with anyone that has been involved in it and you will find that there were a lot of life lessons around that quilt. If you were fortunate enough to be there, you heard family stories of those before, received some golden nuggets for life, and developed a skill that would keep you warm. You would also be thankful that a loved one thought enough of you to create a labor of love which was the quilt. You gained from the experience of doing the work not just being able to click online. Again, I'm not knocking on technology and innovation. I purchased a weighted blanket online that is so comfortable. But there is something to be said about developing ourselves through experiences that navigate life, which takes me to self-defense.

You can learn situational awareness through brief training, but will you be able to apply it when you need it? Too often, we say we know how to handle it until the threat occurs and then the pressure is on us to respond. That is where continuous training applies. You are only as sharp as you keep your knife. This is aided by your understanding of techniques. It is important to understand things like range of motion, the kinetics of the body, along with concepts of how to apply a technique and generate power. Training for a threat by pressure testing gives you experience with the threat and how to react and respond. Like life, it is not a cookie-cutter approach and anything worthwhile (like a purpose-driven life) will take development. This is how we train in self-defense, specifically in Krav Maga.

Now the real question you have to ask yourself, "Is this all about self-defense with systems like Krav Maga or is this about developing and training myself for life?" And the answer is... YES!

ABOUT THE AUTHOR

Mark Winn is a graduate of Lynchburg University with a Masters Degree in Administration and Bachelors in Applied Communications. He is the owner and operator of Winning Warrior Krav Maga and serves as the chief instructor. He holds instructor level and above in Krav Maga, Traditional Kung Fu & Karate as well as various other Martial Arts over his thirty year journey. He has provided self-defense seminars for domestic violence, law enforcement and various other groups.

He has also obtained personal training certifications

with NASM (National Academy of Sports Medicine), ISSA (International Sports and Science Association) and Training for Warriors under Martin Rooney to improve health which improves life.

He is an entrepreneur who believes that his life is service to others in the businesses he runs. Whether teaching, training or helping people learn how to protect their world through his services, it is about impacting lives. He is married and a father of two.

CPSIA information can be obtained
at www.ICGtesting.com
Printed in the USA
BVHW050133050821
613663BV00003B/12